teen's guides

LIVING
with
THE INTERNET
AND
ONLINE DANGERS

Also in the
Teen's Guides series

Living with Alcoholism and Drug Addiction
Living with Allergies
Living with Anxiety Disorders
Living with Asthma
Living with Cancer
Living with Diabetes
Living with Depression
Living with Eating Disorders
Living with Obesity
Living with Peer Pressure and Bullying
Living with Sexually Transmitted Diseases
Living with Skin Conditions
Living with Sports Injuries
Living with Stress

teen's
guides

LIVING
with
THE INTERNET
AND
ONLINE DANGERS

Corey Sandler

☑Checkmark Books®
An imprint of Infobase Publishing

To William and Tessa, skilled navigators of this brave new digital world

Living with the Internet and Online Dangers

Copyright © 2010 by Word Association, Inc.

Checkmark Books
An imprint of Infobase Publishing
132 West 31st Street
New York NY 10001

Library of Congress Cataloging-in-Publication Data

Sandler, Corey, 1950–
   Living with the Internet and online dangers / Corey Sandler.
     p. cm. — (Teen's guides)
   Includes bibliographical references and index.
   ISBN-13: 978-0-8160-7874-5 (hardcover : alk. paper)
   ISBN-10: 0-8160-7874-2 (hardcover : alk. paper)
   ISBN-13: 978-0-8160-7875-2 (pbk. : alk. paper)
   ISBN-10: 0-8160-7875-0 (pbk. : alk. paper) 1. Internet and teenagers. 2. Internet—Safety measures. 3. Computer security. I. Title.
   HQ799.2.I5S26 2010
   004.67'80835—dc22   2009023137

Text design by Annie O'Donnell
Composition by Hermitage Publishing Services
Cover printed by Art Print, Taylor, Pa.
Book printed and bound by Maple-Vail Book Manufacturing Group, York, Pa.
Date printed: April 2010
Printed in the United States of America

10 9 8 7 6 5 4 3 2 1

This book is printed on acid-free paper.

CONTENTS

Acknowledgments   vi

Introduction   vii

About This Book   ix

1   Is Cyberspace Bad for You?   1

2   Your Online Social Life   13

3   Shopping without Dropping   23

4   Online Job Hunting   38

5   File-Sharing: Free and Frightful   48

6   E-mail Scams and Internet Fraud   55

7   Internet Drugstores   71

8   Finding That Special Someone   75

9   Maintaining Your Identity   86

10   Viruses: A Computer Can Develop a Cold   100

11   Don't Click on That Link   109

12   Cell Phones, IMs, and Text Messaging   116

13   Wireless Security   134

14   How to Help Friends Cope with Internet and Online Dangers   138

Glossary   141

Appendix 1. Helpful Organizations   155

Appendix 2. Text Message Lingo   157

Read More About It   159

Index   160

ACKNOWLEDGMENTS

This book has just my name on the cover, but it could not have reached your hands without the help of many others.

Thanks to James Chambers and Sarah Dalton, who led the editorial team at Checkmark Books/Facts On File as well as Jerold Kappes, who edited the text, and Annie O'Donnell, who designed the book. As he has been for many years, Ed Claflin was captain of my literary ship.

And most of all, thanks to you for reading this book we have all put together. We hope it helps you in dealing with some of the new and sometimes surprising challenges that face teenagers in cyberspace, allowing you to have fun, meet people, and learn . . . in safety.

INTRODUCTION

LIVING WITH THE INTERNET AND ONLINE DANGERS

Here's the thing: In cyberspace, nobody is watching. Also, everybody is watching.

How can both things be true at the same time?

Let's start with the definition of cyberspace. It is not somewhere you go to, like a library or a coffee shop or the mall or the comfortable couch at a friend's house. It is not your computer, your cell phone, the cable or the wireless device that connects you to the Internet, or a Web site. It's actually not a place or a thing at all.

Cyberspace is where the messages and words and instructions you send and the answers headed back to you meet, interact, and change tracks from one destination to another.

When you pick up your cell phone and call one of your best friends, where does that conversation take place? One side is in your hand because that is where your phone is located; the other side is wherever your best friend is standing or sitting. But the conversation is happening somewhere in between, in a stream of codes sent by radio and wire: cyberspace.

The very same thing applies when you are exchanging an e-mail, an instant message, a text message, or a video message with your girlfriend or your boyfriend. The place where the communication is taking place is *out there* in cyberspace.

When you are speaking face-to-face with someone—you still do that from time to time, right?—the connection is direct. You can see the person with whom you are conversing, and he or she can see you. And, for that matter, if there are other people in the room, they can see or hear you.

But most of the time when you're on the Internet or sending a text message from your cell phone, you're clicking away all by yourself. No one is watching both ends of the conversation at the same time. No one is looking out for your privacy or your security or even verifying that the person who is sending you a message is 1) exactly who you think it is, or 2) even a person, for that matter.

And now we come to that other, seemingly contradictory fact: Nobody is watching, and everybody is watching.

Although cyberspace is the most modern of ways to communicate, it is also in many ways the Wild West. There are all sorts of snoops floating around out there in cyberspace. They may be merely annoying, like your little brother who tries to listen on your phone call just to be a pain. They may be nasty jerks who want to infect your computer with destructive viruses. Or they may be criminals who want to steal your money, ruin your reputation, or cause you personal harm.

The biggest problem of all in cyberspace: It is almost impossible to know if someone is listening in or watching where you travel on the Web. Some cell phone calls can be monitored directly or indirectly, and it is also possible to obtain a list of whom you called or who called you. E-mails and text messages are harder to crack—unless someone has managed to steal or guess—your user name and password; if you leave your computer unattended or do not use a sign-on password, any passing friend, family member, or stranger can read your mail.

And then there is this: In most situations, when you use your computer to visit a Web site, the operator of that site (and sometimes even an unrelated snoop) can figure out your computer's location and even a bit about your Internet account.

ABOUT THIS BOOK

It is not the purpose of this book to scare you or to convince you not to use the Internet or a cell phone or other digital device for communication. The fact is that living and playing and working in cyberspace can be a very good experience: full of entertainment, education, shopping, and much of your personal business such as banking or applying for college or for a job.

The not-quite-so-good news is that because cyberspace has become so much a part of our daily lives it has also become the home of some of the same dangers your mother and father and teachers warn you about in the "real world."

One of the first things we are taught as children is "Be careful around strangers." Some of them may want to steal our money. Some may be even more dangerous to us personally.

In writing this book, it is our goal to help you stay safe and secure when you are on the Internet, on your cell phone, or exchanging e-mails, instant messages, text messages, and whatever becomes the next great thing to arrive.

It's okay to go to the big city, and it will be okay to leave your home and go off to college or to your first real job. And it's also okay to launch yourself into cyberspace and see what's going on in the virtual world.

Just be careful out there.

1

Is Cyberspace Bad for You?

The Internet, cell phones, e-mail, text messaging, social networking sites are important and valuable. There are many wonderful things we can all do now electronically that make our lives easier, more fun, and more productive. As a young person, it may be hard for you to even imagine a time when you couldn't listen to your favorite music (or buy a copy of a hot new track) anywhere or anytime without having to go to a store. And you are completely comfortable with the idea that a good part of your social life can happen in cyberspace. You can keep up with your friends, meet new ones, and hang out online through a keyboard, a microphone, or a webcam. You can send a detailed e-mail, dash off a quick text message, or alert your circle of friends and followers about the latest details of lunch.

Something else to keep in mind: There are some nasty and ugly people in this world. They're on the street, they're at the mall, they may be in your school, and they're certainly lurking in the dark corners of cyberspace. We'll spend a great deal of time in this book discussing the dangers online and the ways you can protect yourself.

Not long after the telephone was first brought into homes in the 1880s, there were con artists and other crooks who found ways to invade people's privacy and their bank accounts.

Before that time, there were plain old letters in envelopes. We know there were problems with fraud and theft because the deputy postmaster general Benjamin Franklin appointed an inspector in

1772; the Postal Inspection Service is one of the oldest federal law enforcement agencies in the United States.

In other words, we'll also keep telling you that the whole idea of online communication is not evil or dangerous all by itself.

And then there is the question that many parents and teachers and some teenagers themselves ask: Is it healthy to spend all day, every day, playing video games or surfing the Net or sending IMs?

The Internet Is an Essential Nutrient

Put this one in your back pocket and have it ready the next time someone else calls you a slacker for spending all that time on the Internet.

"It might surprise parents to learn that it is not a waste of time for their teens to hang out online," according to Mizuko Ito of the University of California, Irvine. Ito was the lead author of what may have been the most detailed study of American teens and their use of digital media. The study, released in November 2008, was supported by the John D. and Catherine T. MacArthur Foundation's $50-million digital media and learning initiative.

That major foundation is exploring how the Internet and other digital media are changing the ways young people learn, play, socialize, and participate in civic life.

"There are myths about kids spending time online, that it is dangerous or making them lazy," said Ito. "But we found that spending time online is essential for young people to pick up the social and technical skills they need to be competent citizens in the digital age."

Bottom line: Cyberspace is becoming more and more part of our world, and young people are learning how to navigate there as they grow up rather than having to change their habits as adults.

Ito led a team of researchers at the University of Southern California and the University of California, Berkeley. Over three years, they interviewed more than 800 young people and their parents and spent more than 5,000 hours observing teens on sites such as MySpace, Facebook, YouTube, and other networked communities.

The researchers identified two distinctive categories of teen engagement with digital media: friendship-driven and interest-driven. While

This is another example of an area where the world has changed tremendously in the lifetimes of just a few generations. There was a time when people worried that young people were working too hard in the fields or in factories and not getting enough time in school or at play.

There were times when experts said that youngsters were too involved in football or baseball or tap dancing or other activities

friendship-driven participation centered on "hanging out" with existing friends, interest-driven participation involved accessing online information and communities that may not be available from friends or locally.

The study found that adults tend to be in the dark about what youth are doing online and often view online activity as risky or an unproductive distraction. On the other hand, young people understand the social value of online activity and find it very much worth their time to participate. The study found that teens respect one another's authority online and are more motivated to learn from one another than from adults.

"Online spaces provide unprecedented opportunities for kids to expand their social worlds and engage in public life, whether that is connecting with peers over MySpace or Facebook, or publishing videos on YouTube," said Ito. "Kids learn on the Internet in a self-directed way, by looking around for information they are interested in, or connecting with others who can help them. This is a big departure from how they are asked to learn in most schools, where the teacher is the expert and there is a fixed set of content to master."

On the down side, Ito and her group said that not all young people are taking advantage of the educational opportunities on the Internet. And there is also the problem that messages, profiles, pictures, and videos posted online by young people can—and do—end up being viewed by people outside of their own circle and can be difficult or impossible to remove from the Internet.

More information about the study and the MacArthur Foundation's digital media and learning initiative is available online at www.digital-learning.macfound.org.

and not devoting enough attention to school. When television came along—you guessed it—it was argued that valuable time in the library was being missed.

The real answer is very much like what your school nurse or the lunchroom lady may have told you about your diet. There's nothing particularly wrong with having an occasional piece of candy or an orange or a greasy cheeseburger; where you will run into problems with your health is if that is all you eat. You need a balance of fruits and vegetables and protein, and there's probably a bit of room for an occasional Twinkie.

In the online world, there is no evidence that spending time on the Internet or a cell phone or watching television all by itself is bad for you. There have even been scientific studies on the subject. (Here's a job you might want to consider after your graduate: playing video games and watching TV.)

But you do need to get a life, and you have to be as careful online as you would be walking on the street or going to the bank or meeting new people.

As a young adult, that means a mix of time online, plus activities that bring you together with real people, and a bit of action like playing a sport. You know: fruits, vegetables, protein, and keeping a tight hold on your wallet, your privacy, and your personal safety.

HOOKED ON THE NET

For most users, the Web is just part of a well-rounded life that includes both a cyber world and a real world. The Internet can be helpful and educational and fun. But for some, it can also be every bit as much of an obsession as drug addiction, alcoholism, and other problems.

Dr. Kimberly Young, a professor at St. Bonaventure University in upstate New York, is an internationally known expert on Internet addiction and online behavior. Dr. Young serves as the director of the Center for Internet Addiction Recovery. She conducts seminars on the impact of the Internet and is the author of *Caught in the Net.*

Here are some of the questions Dr. Young says you should ask yourself:

"Is the Internet causing a problem in your life? Have other people complained about it?"

"Have your parents tried to put restrictions on your use of the Internet? Have you failed to meet those restrictions?"

"Do you find you sneak online in the middle of the night?"

There is nothing wrong with the Internet itself, according to Dr. Young. The bigger issue is how it affects a young person's life.

"If you don't already have relationships and you're only doing MySpace and Facebook and online games and only communicating through the Internet, you're not developing the social skills you will need to participate in groups and teams."

On the other hand, according to Dr. Young, if the Internet is just part of the things you do—along with participating in sports and clubs at school—you're learning how to relate to people.

"The students that I see in college now are very different than they were five years ago," Dr. Young said. "They're growing up with the technology, and many start experiencing problems when they do team projects; they don't know how to handle that very well."

It comes back to the question of a balanced diet. "The problem with the Internet comes when your online world becomes your social life," Young said.

"Recognizing that there is a problem is a big step. Talk to your parents, to your teachers or a guidance counselor, or someone else you feel comfortable with."

BE CAREFUL OUT THERE

Jill thinks that she may have met the guy of her dreams. Actually, she hasn't really met him; they've only been exchanging messages in a chat room and sending quick little text messages. CUL8TR, she told him.

Jack told her he was, like her, 16 years old and in high school, and he seemed so shy and vulnerable. When he signed one message HAK—hugs and kisses—Jill was thrilled.

But what Jill doesn't know is that Jack is not 16, not in high school, and not the guy of her dreams. He is a dangerous sexual predator, trolling the Internet hoping to find a young girl who would be fooled into accepting his offer to CUL8TR, to see him in a place of his choice.

DANGERS ONLINE

You wouldn't leave your money and your cell phone sitting on a park bench while you go climb a tree, right? If someone you don't trust asks you for the combination to your locker at school, you're smart enough not to give it, correct?

If you're home alone and someone you don't know is rattling the doorknobs and looking into the windows, you'd call the police. And

Are You Addicted to the Internet?

How do you know if you're already addicted or rapidly tumbling toward trouble? Dr. Young has developed the Internet Addiction Test, reprinted here (with modifications) by permission.

For more information, consult the center's Web site at www. netaddiction.com.

To assess your level of addiction, put a circle around the appropriate numbered answer for each question; leave the question blank if it does not apply to you.

1. How often do you find that you stay online longer than you intended?

   1=Rarely 2=Occasionally 3=Frequently 4=Often 5=Always

2. How often do you neglect household chores to spend more time online?

   1=Rarely 2=Occasionally 3=Frequently 4=Often 5=Always

3. How often do you prefer the excitement of the Internet to spending time with your friends?

   1=Rarely 2=Occasionally 3=Frequently 4=Often 5=Always

4. How often do you form new relationships with fellow online users?

   1=Rarely 2=Occasionally 3=Frequently 4=Often 5=Always

5. How often do others in your life complain to you about the amount of time you spend online?

   1=Rarely 2=Occasionally 3=Frequently 4=Often 5=Always

6. How often do your grades or schoolwork suffer because of the amount of time you spend online?

   1=Rarely 2=Occasionally 3=Frequently 4=Often 5=Always

7. How often do you check your e-mail before something else that you need to do?

   1=Rarely 2=Occasionally 3=Frequently 4=Often 5=Always

8. How often does your job performance or productivity suffer because of the Internet?

   1=Rarely 2=Occasionally 3=Frequently 4=Often 5=Always

9. How often do you become defensive or secretive when anyone asks you what you do online?

   1=Rarely 2=Occasionally 3=Frequently 4=Often 5=Always

10. How often do you block out disturbing thoughts about your life with soothing thoughts of the Internet?

    1=Rarely 2=Occasionally 3=Frequently 4=Often 5=Always

11. How often do you find yourself anticipating when you will go online again?

    1=Rarely 2=Occasionally 3=Frequently 4=Often 5=Always

12. How often do you fear that life without the Internet would be boring, empty, and joyless?

    1=Rarely 2=Occasionally 3=Frequently 4=Often 5=Always

13. How often do you snap, yell, or act annoyed if someone bothers you while you are online?

    1=Rarely 2=Occasionally 3=Frequently 4=Often 5=Always

14. How often do you lose sleep due to late-night log-ins?

    1=Rarely 2=Occasionally 3=Frequently 4=Often 5=Always

15. How often do you feel preoccupied with the Internet when off-line, or fantasize about being online?

    1=Rarely 2=Occasionally 3=Frequently 4=Often 5=Always

(continues)

(continued)

16. How often do you find yourself saying "just a few more minutes" when online?

    1=Rarely 2=Occasionally 3=Frequently 4=Often 5=Always

17. How often do you try to cut down the amount of time you spend online and fail?

    1=Rarely 2=Occasionally 3=Frequently 4=Often 5=Always

18. How often do you try to hide how long you've been online?

    1=Rarely 2=Occasionally 3=Frequently 4=Often 5=Always

19. How often do you choose to spend more time online over going out with others?

    1=Rarely 2=Occasionally 3=Frequently 4=Often 5=Always

20. How often do you feel depressed, moody, or nervous when you are off-line, which goes away once you are back online?

    1=Rarely 2=Occasionally 3=Frequently 4=Often 5=Always

After you've answered all the questions, add the numbers you have circled for each response to obtain a final score. The higher your score,

you would never get into a car or do anything but walk away from a stranger who approaches you on the street.

That's because you're smart—street smart, home smart, school smart.

But wait—there's a whole other world out there: the Internet, text messaging, chat rooms, cell phones. And almost everyone old enough to go shopping now has a debit card or a credit card: plastic money.

the greater your level of addiction and the problems your Internet usage causes. Here's a general scale to help measure your score:

20–49 points: You are an average online user. You may surf the Web a bit too long at times, but you have control over your usage.

50–79 points: You are experiencing occasional or frequent problems because of the Internet. You should consider their full impact on your life.

80–100 points: Your Internet usage is causing significant problems in your life. You should evaluate the impact of the Internet on your life and address the problems directly caused by your Internet usage.

After you have identified the category that fits your total score, look back at those questions for which you scored a 4 or 5. Did you realize this was a significant problem for you?

Say you answered 5 (always) to Question #14 about lost sleep due to late-night log-ins. Have you ever stopped to think about how hard it has become to drag yourself out of bed every morning? Do you feel exhausted at school? Has this pattern begun to take its toll on your body and your overall health?

Used with permission from Dr. Kimberly Young, Executive Director of the Center of Internet Addiction Recovery. Available at www.netaddiction.com.

But just because cyberspace is virtual, that does not mean that there are not real dangers out there. The same sort of bad people who can cause problems for people in the "real" world are also lurking on the Internet. They spend their time looking for ways to steal your money, ruin your name, or even cause you harm.

Sometimes the threat is to your reputation: gossip and lies, or revealing something deeply personal about you that you want to keep to yourself. And there are people who will lie to you over the

Internet, pretending to be your friend or your soul mate or a doctor or a teacher, and then tell the world your secrets.

Do you have your own page on a personal Internet site? Do you share your most personal thoughts in a blog there? Is there a real chance that outsiders could break in and read your page? And if you ever change your mind about something you wrote, is there any way to get back your private life? Don't count on it.

Have you ever filled out a job application online? Have you given personal information to a store you've visited online? Are you beginning to think about applying for college? Have you ever entered a contest for free music, games, or concert tickets and revealed your name, age, telephone number, and maybe a little bit about your personal likes and dislikes? Have you ever inquired about a summer job online?

Have you ever visited a Web site—on purpose or by accident—that your mom or dad, your friends, or the police might not consider appropriate? Or perhaps you went to a site to research something that is important to you for some deeply personal reason. Did you realize that the owner of the Web site can record your computer's electronic address? Who controls the information you provided?

When you turn off your computer, do you think that the "history" of your Web browsing fades away as the screen goes black? The truth: Most computers store a record of your history of virtual travel on the Internet. And the Web sites you have visited may place hidden "cookies" on your machine to help them identify you or keep track of things you have done. And even if you clean up your own computer to delete your browsing history and erase all cookies, your Internet provider may keep track of all of your actions on its own system.

The personal e-mail and instant message to your best friends may seem to disappear off your screen when you click on the send button. But copies of the mail can end up in dozens of places in cyberspace as the message is bounced from place to place; in most situations, your mail is sent like an open letter, and there is no real guarantee of privacy.

If you've got a cell phone, somewhere out there in cyberspace is a record of all of the calls you have made or received, plus all of the messages that have gone back and forth. If you visit the Web site for the company that provides your cell phone service, you can see all of the calls you made and the ones you received. If your parents are paying the bill, they can read the same report. This may not be a big deal, unless there is something on that record that you consider your own private business.

THE WILD WEB

In 2008, a Missouri woman accused of taking part in a MySpace hoax that ended with a 13-year-old girl's suicide was indicted on federal charges of conspiracy and accessing protected computers without authorization to get information used to inflict emotional distress. According to prosecutors, the St. Louis woman helped create a fake MySpace account to convince the girl she was chatting with a nonexistent 16-year-old boy. Megan Meier hanged herself at home in October 2006, allegedly after receiving a dozen or more cruel messages, including one stating the world would be better off without her.

Trusting an Adult

Although all young persons want to be able to handle all of their problems by themselves, that's not always possible, and it is certainly not always necessary. Sometimes you've just got to find an adult you can trust to help you deal with something new, something difficult, or something threatening.

First, many adults have a great deal of experience in dealing with government agencies, law enforcement, and (alas) the small but annoying percentage of people who are crooks, criminals, and vandals.

Second, some problems involving banks, credit card companies, contracts, and medical concerns require the involvement of an adult. This may be very much to your benefit in fighting off frauds who try to take advantage of you.

And, if you become involved in getting together in person with someone you have only met online—or if you are going to have direct contact with someone for the purchase or sale of an item—you really need someone at your side to protect you. Think of the person as your wingman or wingwoman.

Throughout this book, certain situations described are best resolved by talking to or seeking help from a trusted adult. If you're not comfortable enlisting a member of your own family, ask someone else: a friend of the family, a teacher or guidance counselor, a member of the clergy, or a law-enforcement officer. They'll be glad you asked.

A grieving father in England has attacked Web sites offering advice on suicide after his teenage son trawled the Internet for information on the best way to kill himself. Tim Piper, a bright student, was found hanged in a closet in his bedroom. His parents had no idea that their son had been logging on to Internet sites filled with information on the easiest way to commit suicide.

In 2008, the personal e-mail and cell phone voicemail accounts of a presidential and vice presidential candidates were hacked by outsiders, and the accounts of more than a few celebrities were also broken into and some of the information published. In 2009, the supposedly private Twitter accounts of prominent politicians, news anchors, and celebrities suddenly began displaying "news" that was not true and not at all flattering.

WHAT YOU NEED TO KNOW

▸ Cyberspace is neither bad nor good; it is an extension of the real world that has some beautiful and ugly things and both good-hearted and evil people.

▸ There is fraud and crime both inside and outside of cyberspace. Part of growing up and becoming independent is learning how to keep yourself safe and secure and how to deal with problems when they happen.

▸ Spending all of your time in the virtual world is not good for your health; you need to get out and experience the real world too. The same goes for playing video games, watching television, and playing football. You need a life with variety and change.

2

Your Online Social Life

Once upon a time, if you wanted to make a record of your deepest most personal thoughts, hopes, and fears, you might have bought a little book and started page one in this way: "Dear Diary." And then you would have taken that diary and clicked it shut with a little lock and put it inside a box. Finally, you'd cover it with six sweaters and maybe some old gym socks and hide it in a place where your 'rents or your little brother or Freddy Krueger could not possibly find it and read it.

Today, though, you just might do this instead: Turn on your computer and use the Internet to go to a Web site known to millions of other people. There you would create (for free) a page of your very own and tell the world your name, your age, your address, your telephone number, and how to reach you by e-mail.

And then you might decorate your personal page with details about your wishes and hopes and fears: what you're looking for in a boyfriend or a girlfriend, the things that make you happy or sad, and the most intimate 411 about yourself and your friends. Oh, and you would probably add a few pictures.

If this were a perfect world, the idea of Facebook or MySpace or any of dozens of other social network Web sites would be pretty cool and quite harmless. They would offer a chance for you to come out of your shell as a young adult and explain yourself to your friends and perhaps even add a few more people to your circle.

When it comes time for you to apply to a college or for a job, you'll be doing pretty much the same sort of thing: putting yourself and your experiences in a neat package and presenting it to someone else to evaluate, hoping they'll pick you.

In a less formal way, you do something like this when you meet someone in a social situation: You select the clothing and arrange your hair and do whatever else you do to show the image you want to present. And then you polish your lines so that the people you meet want to include you in their world.

WHAT COULD POSSIBLY GO WRONG?

Alas, as we're going to point out many times in this book, this is not a perfect world. The fact is that your school, your neighborhood, your town—the world—is not always an honest and fair place. We are surrounded by *posers*, people who put forth a "package" that is not always true.

In the simplest and least threatening situation, these posers are no more dangerous than anyone else who seeks to boost himself or herself above what they really are. You already know these kinds of people: the guy who claims to have a Porsche but keeps showing up at parties on a bicycle, or the girl who claims to be *this close* to half a dozen TV hearththrobs. Yeah, sure . . . but no harm done.

And then, unfortunately, there are real threats. Imagine that on MySpace you become friends with a cute 18-year-old guy whose page says he is headed off to Syracuse University on a combined lacrosse and creative writing scholarship and plays lead guitar in a hot country western/hip hop fusion band. Sounds very promising.

Except, how do you know "JoJo" is not really a 45-year-old unemployed school cafeteria janitor with a criminal record who lives in his parents' basement? The answer is: You don't, unless you step outside of the virtual world of the Internet and make actual contact. And before you do step outside, be sure that you know how to protect yourself in the real world.

THINGS YOU NEED TO KNOW ABOUT SOCIAL NETWORKING

Keep private things private. Don't imagine that anything you post on a Web site will remain private. Always assume that someone out there will find a way to read it. And one more very important thing to remember: Whether you like it or not, someone out there could decide to make use of your photo or your writing or your name in ways you never imagined or wanted. It may not be legal, but that doesn't seem to matter to some people.

Don't embarrass yourself. Here's a pretty good rule to follow: Don't put anything online that you wouldn't want your parents, your best friends, your worst enemies, a college admissions officer, a potential employer, the police, or anyone else to see. If someday you win *American Idol* or are signed to a $25 million contract to play professional baseball, would you like a reporter to find your old Facebook page and show it to the world?

Always assume someone will notice. Do you really want everyone to see that picture? Will you feel the same way in 10 years? You may look really great in your new outfit or bathing suit. That picture of you at the party where you made that strange face and held a can of beer in your hand—whether you drank it or not—may seem funny now, but would you want a college admissions officer or an employer to see it? Remember: Once you post something online, you stand a good chance of losing control of the ownership of the picture.

Use security settings wisely. Take the time to set privacy rules for your page. Most social Web sites (MySpace and Facebook included) allow you to make your page private or public. Do you really want everyone to be able to read your profile and contact you, or do you want to be able to invite only those people you know and accept invitations from friends? If you make your profile "public," you should assume that you're going to hear from strangers.

(Some social Web sites give you more options than others in setting privacy levels. Others automatically make Web pages private for users under the age of 16, for example; they are relying, though, on people being honest about their age when they sign up.)

Here's a tip for the careful but adventurous type: Create both a public and private page and maintain separate e-mail addresses for each. You can relax (a little) on your private page, and you can keep a cautious eye on the public one. If the public page (and its separate e-mail address) start to fill up with garbage, you can close down the page and e-mail account.

Keep a low profile. Don't give out information that strangers have no need to know. Keep your phone number to yourself. Don't list your home address or post a picture in front of your house or your school or someplace recognizable, and don't reveal details that might allow someone to figure out how to find you.

Like what? If you say in your profile that you love to hang out at Smiley's Ice Cream Parlor every Thursday night after bowling at

Hometown Lanes, you might be giving a creep enough information to find you without your permission.

You might not give the name of your school in your profile, but did you pose in a uniform or with a T-shirt that gives a lurker enough information to figure out where you are?

Reveal your information with care. If you decide that someone you meet online is worth meeting on the phone, you can give out your number without telling the entire world. In fact, it might be better to ask the other person to give you his or her phone number first; they can send you an e-mail with the information.

You may be able to find out some information about the person just by entering his or her phone number into a Web browser like google. com. The first place you may end up visiting is an online phonebook, which may tell you the name and address of the person who owns that number; this usually works only for regular phones and not cell phones. You might also find newspaper articles or other references by entering someone's full name into a browser. The best way to do this is to use the full name in quotes so that the whole name is matched.

Be truthful about your age. Don't say you are 18 if you're really a few years younger. For that matter, don't say you're 18 if you're 17 years and 11 months old; there is a big difference in many states that affect the rights and responsibilities of minors and adults.

The same goes the other direction. If you are 18 years or older, or in some situations at least 21 years old, don't say you are younger. That's not fair to younger people, and it may be enough—all by itself—to get you in trouble with the law.

Don't tolerate hate. If someone is spewing garbage about someone else or about a group of people who have a particular skin color, ethnic background, religion, sexual orientation, disability, or some other personal matter, don't just turn the page. If you know the person who is making the comments, you might want to engage him or her in a conversation. You don't have to get personally involved, either, but you shouldn't just ignore the person: Report the comments to the operator of the Web site.

If it feels wrong, it is wrong. If something makes you uncomfortable or scared, let the operators of the Web site know about it. Threats of violence or encouragement to commit crimes are never appropriate, and you just might help prevent something bad from happening by alerting the operator of the Web site or the police or your parents. The same applies for pornography or sexual matters; there may be a place for that sort of thing somewhere, but if what you see is something that disturbs you, then you are either visiting the wrong type of Web site or someone is violating the rules for what should be a safe place. Again, tell the Web site owners or a trusted adult.

Sex may get you the wrong kind of attention. There's flirting, there's romance, there's true love, and there's sex. Things don't always happen in that order, and in any case, not everyone is ready for something heavy while still in their teens.

Make sure that you are on a comfortable level with someone you meet in a social network. Don't post an R-rated photo unless you want to receive R-rated (or X-rated) responses—and if that is what you want, ask yourself why you would be doing that on a public or semipublic Web site.

The same goes with any comments you make in your profile. If you're a young teen, talk about things that young teens are interested in, and don't try to sound as if you are much older than you are.

Learn to read between the lines of any messages you receive. Are you putting out "let's be friends" vibes and getting back "let's be lovers" responses? Is someone saying something to you because they mean it, or because they are trying to fool you into believing something else?

And don't lead someone on, either. The best use of a social network site is to meet people and develop friendships. Don't talk about sex with a stranger; remember, you don't really know who the other person really is, and for that reason you should keep your most personal thoughts, experiences, and dreams to yourself.

Be careful out there. If you do make the decision to meet face-to-face with someone you have met only online, do it carefully and on your own terms. You should choose the place. Make it somewhere public and safe. Bring a friend or an adult you trust. Even better, tell your parents and give them all the details; maybe they'll promise to come along and stay in the background.

Don't be a sucker. You do know Santa Claus is not real, right? Well, the same thing goes for people who offer you things that seem too good to be true. If someone contacts you out of the blue to tell you that he wants your help in safely redepositing $10 million in unclaimed money from a relative/client/prisoner in Nigeria/Iraq/Serbia, you should ignore/forget/delete the message or anything like it.

Do not send your debit card number or your bank account number or any other information. If someone is badgering you with this sort of thing, notify your Internet provider or your cell phone company or the police or ask a trusted adult for assistance.

The same thing goes for strangers who somehow get your e-mail or IM address or your phone number and offer to sell you expensive items at cheap prices. Although you will find great prices at reputable Web sites, you will rarely find a bargain in an e-mail that comes unrequested from an unknown person. "Replica" watches or handbags are usually cheap junk. Even more dangerous is buying medicine from strangers; never buy drugs without a prescription from your own doctor, and always assume that a "pharmacy" selling prescription medications by junk mail is only out to help themselves. At best, the medicines they sell may be useless sugar pills; at worst, they could be dangerous fakes or could get you in trouble with the law.

Watch out, too, for fraudulent "phishers" who pose as someone else or as a bank or credit card company and try to get your personal information. They're trying to rip you off. Stop and think: The bank already has your information—they're not going to ask you to give it to them again. If you get a message asking for this sort of stuff, don't respond; if they say they're from your bank, let's say, call the bank at the phone number you find on the statement you get in the mail or on the back of your debit or credit card and ask them about the message.

And if you think you may have been victimized, call or visit your bank or call your credit card company using the number you find on the card. You can also ask the police or visit a real bank and ask for their assistance.

Stop before you click again. If you receive an e-mail from someone you don't know and it asks you to click on a link to visit a Web site, stop. Any time you do something like that you are opening yourself up to the possibility that a nasty virus will be headed your way. Just remember: If you don't know or trust the person or company that is asking you to "click here" or download a file, just say no.

SOCIAL NETWORK SAFETY NETS

MySpace, at least for the moment, claims the title as the most popular social networking site, with about 247 million members. Facebook is also huge but had about half as many registered users, some 124 million at the start of 2009.

Reporting Inappropriate Behavior

Nearly every social networking site has a process that allows you to report or "flag" a comment or a message that you find offensive or inappropriate. For example, in MySpace, look for the Contact MySpace section and select "Reporting Abuse."

If someone makes a direct threat against you, be sure to tell a trusted adult. If you have any reason to believe this person may know who you are and how to find you, you should notify the police or other law-enforcement agencies.

And if you think you see a person threatening to hurt himself or herself or someone else, you should also discuss the matter with a trusted adult. You might save someone who is crying out for help, and that's a good thing.

Other big players, along with their estimated membership, include Friendster (90 million) and Classmates (50 million). Sites popular in the United Kingdom, Europe, and other parts of the world include Habbo (100 million), Orkut (67 million), Bebo (40 million), and Badoo (13 million).

Most of the major sites offer a pretty flexible collection of safety features and settings intended to protect users from being contacted by people without their permission and to keep a tight lid on the privacy of personal profiles. Some work better than others, and none of them will work if you don't follow safety recommendations or keep your password and user name secret.

Following are some of the settings offered by MySpace and Facebook; other sites offer similar choices.

Private Profile. If you choose to make your profile "private," then only those people you give permission to can see the details and other information you list. Your home page, though, will be viewable by anyone; anything listed there should be something you don't mind the world seeing. Depending on the service you use, you may be able to limit viewing only to your "friends" or those you include in your "network."

In Facebook, you can limit the ability of others to see just about any individual piece of information. And you can also click on the instruction to "see how a friend sees your profile" to examine the effect of privacy settings you have made; make sure that items you want to remain hidden cannot be seen.

Do you want anyone to be able to see your home page, or just those on your friends list? If you allow anyone to find you, do you want to allow him or her to send you a message? Do you want them to see your list of friends? (If you allow strangers to see the names or screen names of your friends, you might end up allowing someone to get in touch with you through the back door. For example, one of your friends may be less concerned about security than you, and they might be fooled into revealing your e-mail or telephone number to a stranger who claims to know you.)

Block Another User. If you are contacted by someone you do not know or someone you do not want to hear from, you can prevent the person from attempting to reach you through the social network. To do this in MySpace, you need to go to the page of the user who has contacted you and find the "Block User" link; click on it and confirm this is what you really want to do.

And please realize that blocking someone within a social network does not do anything to prevent someone from contacting you if they have your e-mail address, your street address, or your telephone number.

If you are concerned that this person is a threat to your personal safety or may commit other crimes, you should immediately discuss the situation with your parents or a trusted adult or contact your local police department. MySpace and most other social network sites also ask you to notify them through their "Contact" link so they can assist.

Preapprove Comments. Unless you change this setting, any of your friends or others who are able to see your page can leave a comment. If you want to be able to look at all comments and decide whether or not they should be allowed to be displayed, turn on "pre-approve comments."

Turn Off the "Online Now" Icon. Most networks, including MySpace, automatically notify anyone who visits your page if you are online now and available to chat. If you would rather not announce that, go to account settings and remove the check mark next to "Show People When I'm Online."

Limit Your Announcements. Many social Web sites allow you to automatically notify your friends of changes to your page such as new photos or new comments, or to alert them when someone is added as a friend or taken off your list of friends. On Facebook, you can adjust the privacy settings of the "News Feed" and the "Wall" to make these actions visible—or not—to those within your circle. Other sites offer similar settings.

Remove Public Search Listing. Many social Web sites submit the names of all of their members to search engines; that means if someone enters your name into Google or another site like it, your MySpace or other page will be listed. The listing on search engines is usually very limited, with just your name and your picture if you have submitted one; some listings will also show the names of some of your friends.

Facebook and some other services allow you to remove your name from search engine listings. If this is your desire, be sure to choose that option when you first set up your home page. Once you are listed on a search engine, it is very difficult—maybe impossible—to wipe out all records of your presence if you change your mind later.

Facebook and other sites promise that pages created by minors— those younger than 18 (or 16 in some places)—will automatically not be submitted to search engines.

Dangerous Widgets

Most social networking sites now allow you to install "widgets" or "gadgets" or other little programs to run on your page. For example, you might want to add a chorus line of dancing elves, or a video of the day from a comedy site, or the weather report; every day there are more and more of these widgets available.

Although the vast majority of these little programs pose no risk to you, here is the problem: When you install a new widget, you are giving its maker access to your profile. If just one out of a thousand, or one out of ten thousand decides to invade your privacy, it's out of your control. And, to go one step further, if some nasty person manages to get into the computer of one of the distributors of a widget, that person could insert a virus or spyware.

WHAT YOU NEED TO KNOW

▸ Social networking sites are great places to meet people without actually having to meet them. Use them to explore your personality and learn about other people.

▸ Never put anything on a social network Web site that you wouldn't show to your grandmother, or a college enrollment officer, or someone who may consider you for a job years from now. Remember that anything you post on the Internet can get completely out of your control, and you may never have the chance for a do-over.

▸ Learn about and use the security settings on a social network site. You might want to start out being as private as you can be, only allowing the friends you choose to see your page. You can always loosen the settings later.

▸ Do not reveal private information to the public. That includes your real name in most cases, your phone number, your address, and your e-mail information. You can always choose to make direct contact with someone later, but start out by keeping everything within the Web site.

▸ If you do choose to meet someone in person after a social network introduction, be very cautious. Make sure to tell all the details to a mature friend or a trusted adult. Have the meeting in a public place, and keep it short and simple.

▸ Always remember that if something feels wrong, it probably is wrong. Don't put yourself into an uncomfortable position on purpose, and if you find yourself creeped out or scared, end the relationship quickly and tell a trusted adult all the details.

3

Shopping without Dropping

When personal computers were first introduced, about 1980, there were only a few things you could do with them: simple word processing, basic math and accounting, and a handful of very simple games. And when cell phones became the next great thing later in that decade, they were pretty good at one thing: making and receiving calls.

With each of these devices, it was hard to imagine at the time that they would both become essential tools to allow us to go shopping for just about anything, anywhere, at anytime. Today, though, this is one of the most common and useful tasks we perform with our computers and our cell phones.

That's not to say that everything always goes well. It takes a certain amount of trust to buy something without seeing it and touching it, and there's also the matter of disclosing your credit, debit, or banking account numbers in an electronic store.

There are four basic ways to go shopping online, and each has its own challenges.

Online outlets of retail stores. This is just a different—and usually more convenient—way to buy something from a store you already know. For example, you can shop at the sites of Sears, Wal-Mart, Best-Buy, and hundreds of other places. Sometimes the prices are the same online as they are at the "brick and mortar" stores with the parking lots and the cash registers, and sometimes they are less. Advantages of dealing with these stores include the fact that you almost always can rely on them backing up their Web sites and their products with the same sort of customer service they offer visitors to the mall.

Online-only stores. Amazon was the first big success here, establishing a place to shop that existed only on the Internet. There is no other way to buy from Amazon (or iTunes or other companies that have the same plan) than at their Web site. Dealing with this sort of company requires you to accept their promises of customer service. And, of course, as we explain in this book, you can also rely on the assistance of your credit card or bank company in disputing fraud or other problems with your purchase.

Third-party stores or auctions. All hail eBay, which invented an electronic business that has made billions in profit without ever having to stock anything in a warehouse. The way eBay works is to serve as a vast, highly organized electronic flea market that matches sellers with shoppers. You could sell your closetful of Beanie Babies or your drawerful of last month's hottest video games without having to speak to or meet the buyer. All you need to do is list the items, send them by mail or delivery service, and collect the money by check or direct deposit into your bank account. As a buyer, you don't have to get up from your chair. There's no need to go to a store or visit some stranger's house; you make your purchase after reading a description and often seeing a picture on a Web site. Operations like eBay and Amazon's Marketplace are often backed by guarantees that the product you buy will be exactly what you expect. And if you use a credit card or a payment service like PayPal (owned by eBay), you also receive protection against fraud or misleading ads. When you visit their Web sites, be sure to read all of the details of the protections offered to buyers at third-party stores before making a bid or purchase.

Person-to-person sales. In the old days, if you wanted to sell a used car or a bicycle, you might purchase a small classified ad in your local newspaper or write up an offer and post it on a bulletin board in a public place. If someone saw your ad and was interested, he or she would call you and discuss the item and perhaps bargain a bit over the price. This sort of direct selling still goes on, although many sellers no longer feel comfortable dealing face-to-face with buyers they don't know. Do you really want someone to call you up and make an appointment to come over to your house and look at your collection of Beanie Babies or the iPod you want to sell? Some people have no problem doing that, while others worry about their personal security or about thieves. (Be sure to consult your parents before inviting a stranger into your house to sell something.)

One company, Craigslist, has become a major player as an online replacement for classified ads. In fact, in many places around the country it carries more ads than do the local newspapers. It is relatively easy to use as either a buyer or a seller, but there is one very important thing to remember about this site and others like it: They are just bulletin boards. They perform little or no investigation of the backgrounds of sellers and the products they offer, and they are not involved with the buyer at all.

ATTENTION EBAY SHOPPERS

There are not that many people on the planet who haven't heard of eBay, and only slightly fewer who have not at least explored the site. You can buy or sell just about anything . . . and people are constantly trying to expand that definition. The ordinary items include electronic devices, jewelry, clothing, software, toys, cars; unusual items that have actually sold include a cooked but uneaten Brussels sprout, a monorail car from Walt Disney World, and a professional arena football team.

The eBay site does not buy, sell, or warehouse anything. All it does is set up and manage a marketplace that brings together buyers and sellers. The company charges sellers for listing their products and takes a piece of the proceeds if a sale is made.

One of the great successes of the Internet, eBay was founded in 1995 as a very casual Web site, and by the end of 2008 it reported worldwide revenues of about $8.5 billion. There are sites in some 30 countries, and eBay also owns the payment processing company PayPal, the Internet telephone service Skype, and the sports and entertainment ticket auction site StubHub.

The company also owns Kijiji, a classified ad service that was started overseas but began operations in the United States in 2007 as a possible competitor to Craigslist. *Kijiji* is a Swahili word meaning "village" and pronounced key-gee-gee.

THE ADVANTAGES OF ONLINE AUCTIONS

Why shop at an online auction site instead of at an online store, or for that matter, at a local retail store? There are two good reasons: First, you just may end up with a bargain. The appeal of an auction is that it offers the most direct connection between supply and demand; the seller says, "How much will you offer me for this?" and you respond, "Here is the most I will pay."

Apples to Apples

When you buy online, make sure you are aware of the full cost of anything you purchase. How much is shipping? Is there an additional handling charge? Does the online site require you to pay sales tax? And finally, if you decide to return the item, is there a restocking fee, and who pays the return postage?

The other good reason is that at times auctions are the only place to find certain very obscure products; think of them as a cyberspace flea market. If, for example, you have a very old computer or camera or toy and need a repair part, you're probably not going to be able to buy it at your neighborhood hardware store. But it is quite possible that someone, somewhere in the world has an extra 6SJ7 sprocket and is willing to sell it to someone at auction.

In the first situation—buying at auction a product also available in stores—before you make a bid, you should do the research to make sure you know the price you would pay if you went to a store (in the mall or online) or dealt directly with a manufacturer. There is absolutely no reason to pay more at auction than you would at a store for the same item.

In the second situation—buying some unusual item from the only seller who possesses the item—you should have a firm idea of how much it is worth to you. One problem many people have at auctions is that they get caught up in the excitement and lose track of the value. It is very easy to say to yourself that a new 6SJ7 sprocket is worth no more than $20 to you and then convince yourself that $22 is only a bit more than $20, and as long as you're bidding why not pay $25 or $30 or $40.

THE RISKS OF ONLINE AUCTIONS

Now consider the disadvantages of buying from an auction site. First, there is the risk that you will pay too much; we've already covered that.

Second, there is the possibility that the item you will be buying will not be new. A used item is just what it sounds like: Someone else has opened the package and worn the clothing or turned on the power switch or read the book. Some used items are nearly perfect, while others may show their history very clearly.

Other products are considered "reconditioned." Have you ever thought about what happens when someone returns an item to a reputable store? A reconditioned item is supposed to be inspected carefully by the seller and, if appropriate, tested to make sure it performs as if it were new. In some situations, the product may have been repaired.

And then there are companies or individuals who are selling an item without permission of the manufacturer; this is sometimes called the "gray market." The product may be new, reconditioned, or used.

Make sure you find out which category items applies. Items that are used, reconditioned, or sold on the gray market may not have a full manufacturer's warranty or may not have any guarantee at all.

Sites such as eBay sound like such simple operations; what could possibly go wrong for you as a buyer or seller? Once again—and you should be used to this by now—the problem is that a few unpleasant people are always looking for ways to cheat, steal, or otherwise ruin a good thing.

There are a number of things you can do to make it more likely that any purchase you make online will meet your needs. Make sure you completely and carefully read the description of the item for sale. Is it new or used? Is it listed as reconditioned? This usually means that it was returned to the store by someone who bought it; it may or may not have required repairs, and it may or may not represent a good deal.

If you're buying an electronic device like a computer, cell phone, or music player, make sure that the seller is offering the latest version of the product. You can usually check this by going to the Web site of the manufacturer. If you're buying a book, see if the seller is offering the most current edition available. There may be nothing wrong with buying an older model of an electronic device or an earlier edition of a book; this is often a way to get a great deal. But do the research and make sure you understand what you are buying. If you are buying software for a computer, though, be sure you find out if the product has a valid license. If you read the fine print on most software (a great way to fall asleep if you need help at night), you'll find that most companies do not sell you ownership of the program; instead, they sell a license that allows you certain rights. The most limited licenses allow you to install the program just once on a single machine and prohibit you from giving or selling the program to anyone else. Other

Pirates Among Us

Some people sell "pirated" software, illegal copies of programs. And others may offer complex schemes where they offer an "update" version of a program along with an older edition that must be installed first. Either way, you may run into problems when you try to register the software with its maker. Registration is required by most software companies to allow them to send you updates and bug fixes ... and to catch (and disable) copies of their product that do not have proper licenses. Be sure you understand what you are bidding on if you try to buy software at auction sites.

forms of licenses require the company to give permission for the software to be transferred from one machine to another.

If you are buying on a Web site such as eBay or Amazon, be sure that you understand as much as you can about the seller. In the case of eBay, remember that all of the products are sold by individuals or companies; eBay doesn't sell anything—it merely serves as a marketplace. On Amazon, some of the products are sold by Amazon itself, while others are offered by other companies and some are used items sold by individuals.

Read the feedback ratings and stay away from sellers that show a history of complaints from buyers. You might also want to stay away from "new" sellers who don't have much of a history; it is possible that they have taken on a new name to hide a connection to a bad history. Let someone else try them out first.

Understand and agree with the terms of the sale. Can you return the item if you change your mind? (Not likely at an auction.) Can you return the item if it is not exactly as advertised? (A legitimate auction site like eBay should back you up in this situation.)

How much are shipping costs, and when can you expect to receive the item? Are there additional "handling" charges? These are usually nothing more than additional profit for the seller. Will the product be shipped immediately? How will it be sent, and when can you expect delivery? Where is it coming from? Add up the cost of the item plus handling charges and shipping; if the total is more than the price at a regular store, you are not getting a bargain at all.

UNDERSTANDING THE AUCTION PROCESS

Make sure you understand how eBay or other online auction works. Here are some of the elements you'll find.

Deadline. An auction, by definition, will have a deadline; the highest bid when the auction closes will usually win the item. Sometimes the best way to win an item is to "lurk" in the background and keep track of the price. If you make an offer early in the process, you may end up raising the final cost because others will respond with their own offers. Some of the most successful bidders make their offers during the last few minutes or seconds before an auction ends.

Reserve price. Some sellers hold on to the right to reject an offer that they consider too low. Most auctions allow sellers to set a "reserve" price, which is the lowest offer they will accept. The listing may or may not tell you if an item has a reserve price.

Buy it now. Some sellers conduct an auction but also list a "buy it now" price. In that case, anyone who offers that amount can win the item immediately. If there is only one of the items offered for sale, the auction ends; if there is more than one item available, others can continue to make offers.

MAKING PAYMENT

The next important issue is deciding how to pay for your purchase. Never use cash. First, it is not safe to send by mail. Second, if someone receives cash and doesn't send a product, you have no protection

Shop in Privacy

Guard the details of your user name and password for any auction Web site. Your account history may include your credit card or bank account numbers as well as your real name, address, e-mail address, and phone number. A thief could steal your identity or could make purchases in your name and have them sent somewhere else.

against loss. Finally, if someone wants to meet you in person and insists you bring cash, be suspicious.

If you use a credit card in making a purchase, the company or bank that issues the card is required by law to protect you against fraud if you follow the rules. Begin by reading the information that came with your card, or call the company and ask them to explain how to protect yourself. In general, you can protest any charge that appears on your monthly statement if you have not received the product you ordered, if it was defective, or if its description was misleading.

Many credit card companies go beyond the basics of federal law and add some sort of satisfaction guarantee for their clients. For example, your card may give you an extended warranty for items you buy or even a period of insurance against breakage or theft. However, the guarantee may not apply to used items or those sold by private parties.

The situation with debit cards varies from company to company. Some offer the same sort of protection you get from a credit card, while others will tell you that using a debit card is very much like writing a check or spending cash: It's up to you to take care of yourself. Call the company or bank that issued you a debit card and ask about the protections it offers.

You are in the strongest position if you make payment through the auction site to the seller. Some online sellers offer their own protections. Read carefully any promise of a guarantee of satisfaction. Some services, like PayPal, which is owned by eBay, offer to guarantee any purchase you make even if it is paid for by direct withdrawal from your checking account. PayPal also is available to buyers at some other online sites.

Keep your financial information away from the eyes of the seller by paying with a credit or debit card or using a guaranteed transfer from your checking account through a service like PayPal. Sellers receive only confirmation that money has been transferred into their account and your name and address for shipping.

Unless you have decided to pay directly to the seller, you should ignore (and report to the auction site) anyone who contacts you directly and asks for information about your banking or debit or credit card information.

If a seller insists on a wire transfer (either directly from your bank or through an electronic money order service like Western Union), you should be very cautious. It may be impossible to get the money back if the product you buy is not delivered or is not satisfactory.

ONLINE AUCTION SCAMS

Just as with other Internet sites, you have to be on guard against people who want to cheat you. Here are four types of auction frauds to beware of: spoofs, siphons, shills, and second-chancers.

Auction Spoofs. If you receive an e-mail that looks like it has come from eBay or another well-known company, that doesn't mean it's for real: it might be a spoof, the electronic equivalent of counterfeit money.

If you receive something like this, start by reading it carefully. It is sometimes very easy to spot a fake e-mail because the senders are often in a foreign country or, sorry to say, they may be kids. How can you figure that out? Look for odd words, spelling errors, and just plain mistakes.

Not to say that a legitimate company won't make an error every once in a while, but if you get an e-mail that says, for instance, "Thank you to being a honoured customer for our esteemed organization," stop and think. The sentence doesn't sound like it was written by someone who is fluent or at least comfortable in English.

But even more important, see what the e-mail is asking you to do. Why would eBay or any other online store ask for your Social Security number, for example? And why would they be contacting you out of the blue to "confirm" your credit card or debit card number?

Why in the world would a place where you have already registered a user name and chosen a password send you an e-mail asking you to reveal them? The purpose of that sort of information is to give you the key to open the door when you visit their Web site. You might have to disclose some information if you were making a purchase, but then you would be contacting the store and not the other way around.

Just as one example, eBay offers a feature called Account Guard, which you can get from their Web site; it installs on your computer and gives you a message to assure you that the eBay site you visit is the real thing.

(You should also make sure you are using the latest version for your Internet browser; current editions include "antiphishing" protection that notifies you if the site you are visiting seems to be properly registered and identified. Among browsers that offer this are current versions of Microsoft Internet Explorer, Mozilla Firefox, and Google Chrome.)

A number of security and antivirus programs, including Symantec's Norton 360 and Norton Internet Security, feature an automatic antiphishing check for each Web site you visit. The program compares the legal registration for the Web site with what the page says it is; if the two don't match up, you'll receive a warning.

Bid Siphoning. If you are participating in an auction, you may receive an e-mail from someone who has figured out who you are, or at least how to reach you with a message. The person may tell you, "I've got the same item for sale, and I will sell it to you for half price if you send money directly to me." The person may claim to be doing this to save having to pay the auction site a commission, which is a reasonable position to take, but the seller may also be just trying to rip you off by taking your money and then disappearing.

If you send money to someone in this sort of arrangement, you have no protection from the auction Web site.

Shill Bidding. A seller might have "shills" placing phony bids. (The word comes from carnivals where a shill tries to convince people to come see a show or buy a trinket).

In an auction, a seller may have one or more friends or partners acting as shills to place bids to drive up the auction price without any intention of buying the item. This is another good reason to wait to place your bid until near the end of an auction period; you can wait to see if the price is still attractive then.

Second-chance Scams. One of the features of eBay and a few other competitors is a "second chance" at buying something even if you did not win it in an auction. Why do they do this? One reason is that sometimes the high bidder fails to pay for an order and the auction is canceled; it might also be that the seller has more than one of the item for sale and is willing to accept your bid. Those are both honest situations.

But just as happens in so many other parts of the Internet world, some people insist on messing up a good thing by trying to cheat the rest of us. According to eBay, some of its customers report receiving fake offers for a second chance.

If you receive an offer at your personal e-mail address, eBay says you should not respond to it and instead go to eBay and sign in and go to My Messages. See if the second-chance offer is listed there and that it was sent to you directly from eBay.

If you have doubts about *any* e-mail you receive that may or may not come from eBay, the company asks that you use your e-mail system to forward the message to a special department that will look at the mail and tell you if it is real. Forward the mail to spoof@ebay.com and wait for a response.

Ebay Safety Tips

Visit this Web page for information on how to safely use eBay: http://pages.ebay.com/securitycenter/mrkt_safety.html

CRAIG'S CLASSIFIED EMPIRE

There really is a guy named Craig, and he started a very successful and profitable business by making a list and putting it on the Internet. That happened in ancient history, in 1995, and Craig Newmark's craigslist.com has gone on to be one of the most popular places to go to if you're looking for a job, a sofa, or even a friend or a date.

In 2009, the company was operating in about 450 locations in some 50 countries, and by some estimates was in ninth place among all U.S. Web sites in visitors. It was receiving more than 30 million new classified ads per month.

The private company is believed to be mostly owned by Newmark, although eBay has a major investment worth about 25 percent of the business.

The good news is that it's free to the person doing the shopping, and free or inexpensive for most people or companies who place the listings. It's also a very easygoing, not very structured Web site.

The bad news is that like almost everything else on the Internet, there are some unpleasant people who try to take advantage of visitors. Some of the products offered for sale may not be exactly as they are advertised, some of the sales are completely phony attempts to rip off buyers, and some of the personal ads are nasty approaches from evil people.

You also have to be careful as a seller. Some scam artists may try to steal from you by engaging in one of many types of phony rackets.

Craigslist is just a middleman in the sale. It does not handle any payments, give any guarantees, or check the true identity of people who post ads on the site. It's all up to you to be careful.

If you receive an e-mail that claims to be from Craigslist and offers some kind of guarantee or a payment service, someone is trying to scam you. You can forward the message to Craigslist (see the section below about contacting the service), and they will advise you of the dangers involved.

Here are some tips from Craigslist; they are also good ideas for any similar online sales site:

1. If someone from far away is contacting you about purchasing a large item, it's probably a scam. It absolutely does not make sense for someone in Africa or Asia or the other side of the country to offer to buy your dirt bike or to sell you a set of barbells. There are local markets for things like that; these kinds of approaches are almost always a scam.

2. On the other hand, if you are selling something that can be shipped through the mail or other delivery service, a safe transaction can be local or far away. There is a certain level of comfort in not having to meet strangers in person.

3. You should automatically reject any offer in which the buyer wants to send you a check for more than the price of the item you are selling and then asks you to send them the difference. There is no reason for someone to do that except to try to get you to give them good money for their phony check.

4. If you do deal with someone local to buy or sell something, get a parent or a trusted and knowledgeable friend to assist you in making the sale. If someone has to come to your house to pick up something or drop it off, make sure your parents are aware of the situation and are there when the money is exchanged.

5. If you receive an e-mail from someone offering to buy something sight unseen, or if someone wants to rent your apartment or become your roommate without ever meeting you, that should also set off alarm bells. This sort of offer almost always involves an attempt to get at your bank account.

6. If you are selling something, never agree to pay in advance by bank transfer or to wire funds by Western Union or any other service like that. If you send the money before you have the product, you may end up with no money and no product.

7. If someone buys something from you, cash is always good. If the person wants to give you a check (or even a cashier's check or money order), you should involve your local bank before you accept payment. There are all sorts of fake checks floating around, and even if your bank accepts the check and deposits it in your account, it can still come back to you later on—even weeks later—and demand the money back if it turns out that the check was no good. You can also use the services of companies like PayPal to

allow an individual to use his or her credit card to pay you. The buyer gets a PayPal guarantee, and you receive good money, minus a service charge.

8. If you are looking for an apartment, make sure that you actually meet the landlord or a rental agent. Never agree to send money for a lease to someone who is out of town or away. If you have any doubts about a lease, ask a trusted adult to assist you in checking with the town or city where the apartment is located to see if there are any reported problems involving the property or the landlord.

CRAIGSLIST PROBLEMS

Because Craigslist is so loosely managed, it is in some ways about as safe as a bulletin board at your local pizzeria. Anyone can put something up on the board, and illegal or improper or fraudulent

Where to Go for Help

If you suspect that an item or service listed on Craigslist may be part of a scam, do not contact the person with the listing but instead send an email to abuse@craigslist.org and include the eight-digit post ID number and other information in your message.

You can also read more advice from Craigslist at this Web page: www.craigslist.org/about/scams

The Federal Trade Commission offers advice and help to consumers who want to know how to shop safely online or who have run into problems. You can call their toll-free Consumer Response Center at 877-FTC-HELP (877-382-4357).

The FTC also has an online complaint form at www.ftc.gov.

The Federal Bureau of Investigation and the National White Collar Crime Center jointly operate a Web site called the Internet Fraud Complaint Center at www.ic3.gov, where you can read about e-mail and other scams and file a complaint.

The Canadian government offers advice about online transactions at the Web site www.phonebusters.com or through its toll-free hotline at 888-495-8501.

listings may or may not be spotted by the company's small staff or its millions of users.

In its defense, Craigslist says it is merely offering that bulletin board service and is not involved in any way in things sold. Whether that is morally or ethically proper is something you might want to debate with your friends or your social studies teacher.

Along the way, Craigslist has run into problems related to the content of some of the postings. Among the issues were ads that appeared to violate civil rights or fair housing laws, "casual encounters" forums that may have been attempts by crooks to obtain personal information about other people, and prostitution rings. There have also been a number of spoofs or gags that have gone wrong, including instances where people have posted ads inviting the public to come and take items from a house that wasn't theirs.

CHECK OVERPAYMENT SCAMS

Wow! Someone is making an offer for the beat-up old guitar you have for sale on a Web site. And even better, instead of offering you the $50 you asked, they want to send you $500. What could possibly be wrong with that deal?

Here's the way this particular scam often works. Crooks have a forged or altered personal check, cashier's check, money order—almost any type of payment you can think of—and they want to fool you into accepting it. They will come up with some kind of story about why the check is so much larger than the amount due; they might claim there was a mistake made at their company or that there was some unusual law that didn't allow them to make it out for the exact amount. None of the stories make any sense.

If you agree to take a check for $500, crooks might tell you something like this: "Keep $50 for your guitar, plus $25 for shipping and another $25 for your trouble in assisting us. Please advise your bank to wire-transfer the remainder, $400, to us immediately. We will be in touch with you later to arrange for shipping the guitar."

If you weren't thinking it through, you might say to yourself: "What have I got to lose? I will get the money in advance, and so I won't be risking sending my guitar and waiting for them to pay. And these guys are going to give me $25 extra just to help them out."

The problem is that in most cases your bank will accept the check you give them for deposit, and it will be a few days before they find out it is a fake or a forgery. In the meantime, if you are following the instructions of the scammers, you will have sent them real money from your account.

When your bank determines the check is not good, they will contact you and take the money out of your account; if you have sent the money to the scammer by wire transfer, those dollars are gone. Even worse, now that they have some of the personal details you gave them, they might try to clean out whatever other money you have in your bank account before they disappear.

The good news—you'll probably still have your junky old guitar; that was never really something the thieves were interested in.

The moral, once again: When something sounds too good to be true, it usually is.

WHAT YOU NEED TO KNOW

- ➤ Shopping online or buying through an Internet auction site can be a great way to save money or find something that is not available locally. But you have to be careful to protect yourself against rip-offs.
- ➤ If you want to make a bid through an online auction, make sure you understand all of the rules. Make sure you know exactly what it is you are bidding on, and don't pay more online than you would at a store.
- ➤ Be sure you understand the total cost of a purchase, including shipping, handling, and sales tax. Some sellers offer a product for a very low price and then jack up the bottom line with unreasonable added charges.
- ➤ Learn as much as you can about a seller. Are there negative ratings posted on a Web site?
- ➤ Do not reveal information to a seller that is not necessary.
- ➤ Do not send cash to someone before receiving a product and inspecting it. If you must pay in advance, use a credit or debit card that offers protections to the buyer or pay through a service that offers a guarantee of satisfaction.
- ➤ Watch out for scams, including auction frauds and check overpayment schemes.

Online Job Hunting

So you're looking for a job? Believe it or not, us old folks used to have buy a newspaper or go to an employment agency or even go from office to office by foot or by phone in search of employment.

Today, though, the Internet has become the fastest-growing doorway to employment. It is quick and easy to search for a job with a few clicks of your mouse; you can search by type of job, by educational requirements, by location, or by most any other detail.

And employers like online applications, too, because they help to quickly deal with what can be a sudden flood of information. Online applications are set up to arrive in a standard form.

Some employers even use computer programs to do the first "read" of applications and résumés. They may be looking for certain high school or college degrees. Or the program may search for specific keywords like manager or engineer. There may be a few specific yes/no questions (such as "Do you have a valid driver's license?" or "Are you fluent in Mandarin?") that might include you in or out of the list of candidates.

This is generally all a good thing. It is usually easier to scan a Web site than to read the classified ads in a newspaper or check the handwritten postings on a bulletin board at your school or an employment office. The Internet sites allow for a much quicker exchange; ads can go up almost immediately, and many sites allow you to apply online.

But there are also some downsides and dangers to using the Internet for your job search. Be sure you understand that not all jobs are posed online; don't limit yourself just to what is quick and easy. When you do apply for a job online, remember that your past may catch up with you. Things you may have done elsewhere on the Internet, such as your postings on a social networking site, may come back to haunt you when you apply for a job.

HOW TO POST YOUR RÉSUMÉ SAFELY

Monster.com, one of the largest online job-search sites, does look into the background and the history of the companies that use its service, although that does not guarantee that every listing is legitimate. The company also advises visitors to its site to beware of fraudulent job opportunities or e-mail that is falsely made to appear as if it came from Monster.

Among the most important bits of advice from Monster involves the care you should take with your résumé. Although it is obviously important that you provide enough information about your educational and work history to attract the interest of an employer, it is also important to do everything you can to keep confidential information away from the eyes of criminals.

Monster advises that online résumés (to their listings or any other job offering) should never include any of the following details:

1. Date of birth. (You can list your age or the year you were born, but leave out the month and date to make it that much harder for a criminal to steal your identity.)
2. Social Security number. (You may need to give your SSN later on in a job interview process if the employer is going to run a background check, and you certainly will need to disclose it for tax purposes if you are hired. But in the initial stages of a job hunt, keep it to yourself.)
3. Driver's license number. (Again, there is no need for this to be listed on a résumé. It may be necessary later on for a background check or as part of your job if it involves driving.)
4. Bank account, credit card, or debit card information. (This information is not needed by an employer in the interview stages of hiring.)
5. User names or passwords. (Again, this information is irrelevant in the initial stages of a job search and for most jobs is never a legitimate interest of the employer.)

Monster.com Safety Tips

To learn more tips from Monster.com, visit this Web page: http://help.monster.com/besafe/

Once an employer invites you to an interview or is preparing to make a job offer, you can disclose personal information that is appropriate. By that time, you should be convinced that the employer and the job opportunity are real. And don't be shy about inquiring, politely and professionally, about the company's policies intended to maintain the privacy of information provided by their job applicants or employees.

BE HONEST AND CONSISTENT

Remember that anything you send over the Internet may (and probably will) end up in an electronic file somewhere else, and that information can easily be reused. So, if you send a résumé to one company or site in which you say you were born in Brooklyn and worked for the past two summers selling shoes, don't send another résumé to another company saying you're from Chicago and spent summers as a computer programmer. One or the other company—or both—may pick up the difference and at the very least ask you to explain the change; at the worst, they may automatically exclude people who seem to have played around with the facts of their résumé.

Sometimes differences from one résumé to another are explainable. You might list Brooklyn on one form and New York City on another; they are both correct since Brooklyn is a part of the city. (The same would be true, say, for Brighton and Boston.) But not every employer knows these details. Try to be consistent so that you do not raise any red flags.

Even more important: Don't inflate your credentials and never lie. If you had a job title; such as assistant to the vice president for human resources, use that label on your résumé. Where things get a bit more difficult is a situation where you had a job without a title; if you sold tickets as well as soda and popcorn at a movie theater, you can list a very general job description like "customer service." But don't make yourself manager. If you get caught in a lie, you're probably not going to be offered a job.

BEHAVE YOURSELF

Remember that slightly naughty photo you posted on your MySpace page? How about the off-color joke you put in your blog? And then there is the silly, just-kidding name you chose for your e-mail account: hunkahunkaburninglove.

Does your profile on MySpace or Friendster or Facebook contain drug references, gangsta boasts, or a list of your 25 favorite beers?

Yes, you were just kidding around. Part of growing up from a kid to a young adult involves trying on some adultlike roles; another part is the desire to try and shock someone by pretending to be something you are not.

But what happens if a possible employer decides to poke around on the Internet to see what it can find out about you?

Companies that are judging candidates for jobs have a pretty common set of questions they need answered before they will offer a job. Do you have the qualifications they seek, have you demonstrated good character, and have you shown mature judgment? Why would someone wanting to be treated as an adult put something out on the Web that demonstrates something else, whether it is truth or fiction?

The more important the job, especially once you are out of high school or out of college, the more likely that an employer is going to

How to Check Up on a Job Applicant

How can a company or a recruiter find out about you if your MySpace page is "private"? Put yourself in their shoes. Don't you think you could find a way to bluff your way into a personal page? Do you automatically reject any inquiries from people seeking to become your "friend"?

And there are other ways: A big employer may hire someone at a college as an intern and then ask that person to check out social network sites using their college ID. The plain fact is that anything that is posted on a Web site may end up being seen by someone you never imagined.

spend at least a bit of time with a Google search and a check of social Web sites like MySpace or Facebook.

In one published survey, executive recruiters were asked if they used search engines to learn more about applicants or fact-check information listed on applications. Of 100 companies surveyed, 77 said they did.

So you have two assignments. First, you need to behave yourself when you are online because you may be leaving a record that will follow you for years. Second, you should spend the time cleaning up your past. Never, ever do anything deceitful like trying to alter entries that are recorded in someone else's system. However, there is nothing wrong with changing your e-mail address, screen name, and profiles to offer a more mature and trustworthy presence to the world.

WATCH OUT FOR PIRATES

Suppose you were a crooked, evil person looking to find out personal information about young people? Think about the information that a job application asks: It starts with your name, address, date of birth, employment history. And then it is not uncommon for some organizations to ask you for your Social Security number.

That combination of information is exactly the sort of information a thief could use to set up a credit card in your name or otherwise pose as you without your permission.

There are four things you can do to protect yourself here.

First, try to deal with online job-hunting sites that maintain at least some level of safeguards. Established job-hunt sites such as Monster. com and Careerbuilder.com have a commercial relationship with the companies offering employment; they charge the firms a fee, and they require them to agree to guarantee at least some level of privacy.

However, if you are dealing with a free job-posting site, there is very little if any checking of the backgrounds of the companies or individuals posting ads. (Craigslist, for example, offers free job listings in some areas and charges minimal fees in others; it requires listers to give a name, address, and e-mail address but does not ordinarily verify the accuracy of the information.)

Second, do some research yourself. If the ad you find online gives you the name of the company, use Google or some other search engine and perform your own investigation. Does the company have a Web site? Is it in the news—with good or bad reports? Do you find postings by others reporting they have been scammed? If something smells fishy, think twice before giving up personal information. Ask someone for advice: a parent, a guidance counselor, or someone else you trust.

Third, don't answer questions that are irrelevant or illegal for an employer to ask. It is against the law for an employer to discriminate on the basis of race or ethnic background, and in general the only relevance of your gender comes in a few very obvious jobs. (Sorry, guys, but you're not going to be hired to be a locker room attendant in the women's changing room at the health club.) Some jobs may require certain physical abilities; a firefighter may have to demonstrate the ability to carry a certain amount of weight or be able to climb a tall ladder. But if you're applying for a job as a babysitter, watch out for someone who asks for a picture or wants to know your dress size. If something looks really wrong, contact the police or a trusted adult.

Finally, if you do respond to a want ad and then find out that someone was trying to scam you (or worse, harm you) don't just walk away. Call the police or ask assistance from a guidance

How One Good Candidate Lost the Job

A few years ago, the *New York Times* published an article about a small consulting company in Chicago interviewing candidates for a summer intern. Before a job offer was made to someone who seemed to be a good candidate, the company went online.

"At Facebook, a popular social networking site, the executive found the candidate's Web page with this description of his interests: 'smokin' blunts' (cigars hollowed out and stuffed with marijuana), shooting people and obsessive sex, all described in vivid slang," according to *Times* education reporter Alan Finder.

The *Times* reported that even though it was evident that the student was posturing—pumping himself up for his friends—they didn't think that sort of image would be appropriate for an employee. He was not offered the job.

The article also quoted Mark W. Smith, assistant vice chancellor and director of the career center at Washington University in St. Louis. "I think students have the view that Facebook is their space and that the adult world doesn't know about it," Smith said. "But the adult world is starting to come in."

counselor or your parents; do this as soon as you realize what has happened. If you have given information like bank account or credit card numbers, contact your bank and report it. You may need to change your account numbers, but you'll be protecting yourself from attempts at fraud.

ONLINE IS NOT THE ONLY WAY TO GET A JOB

By some estimates, only about one-quarter or one-third of all jobs are advertised for filling on sites like Craigslist or Monster.com. Most new hires are made through other means, like direct application to a company or through word of mouth. So don't just sit at your computer: Go out and look for yourself.

THINK LIKE AN EMPLOYER

As you fill out a job application, stop for a moment and put yourself in the chair of the person offering employment. What kind of things would they legitimately want to know before asking you to come in for an interview? And think about what kinds of answers on a form will be a great big red flag that might take you out of consideration.

Here are some of the things employers get suspicious about.

Incomplete academic credentials. If you list a high school or a college, indicate whether you have received a degree. If you say, "Bayside High School, 2005–2009," that raises the question of whether you actually graduated.

Inconsistent or missing references. Some—but not all—employers will contact former supervisors at any previous jobs; most employers want to see that you can list a name and phone number, even if they do not intend to actually call and check up on your history.

If you can list details for your references, go ahead and do so; it wouldn't hurt if you called ahead of time to make sure they are still there and to request permission to list them. If there is a reason why you cannot list a reference for all of your recent employers, give an explanation in the résumé or your cover letter. For example, "My former employer, Ace Speedy Messenger Service, is no longer in business."

Don't assume that employers will call only the references you list or that they might not call a place if you don't provide a name. They might know someone at your former place of work, or they might make a call on their own just to see if there is something they can learn. What's the lesson here? Whatever you really think, never leave bad feelings behind when you depart a job.

Shady business. Don't leave gaps that would make an employer suspicious. For example: a period of several years with no job or school indicated. You're just asking for someone to imagine you were in trouble or that you are omitting a job that didn't work out well.

If you were unemployed or took a job for six weeks selling newspapers while you looked for other work, say so. Include an explanation: "My father was stationed in Paris for two years, and I did not work during that period." Or, "During the period that includes the academic years 2008 and 2009, I was in training for the football team and did not have a job."

If there was a more serious problem, like a brush with the police or a medical problem, you should seek the advice of an experienced professional. Speak with a guidance counselor at your school or with some other adult you trust. Your goal should be to find a way to be honest about who you are, while also demonstrating that you have

---

Fraudulent Job Ads

Does that job offer sound too good to be true? It probably is too good to be true.

While the majority of job postings and "opportunities" listed at online Web sites are legit, you're also going to find a few bad apples in the basket. Some of them are more than just bad, they're downright rotten.

The Federal Trade Commission (FTC), the government agency that monitors commerce and advertising, offers some clues to spotting job ads that may represent frauds or scams. Among the most common categories are schemes involving vending machines, medical billing or transcription, and other work-from-home "opportunities."

In particular, look for ads that promise "quick and easy" or "risk-free" or "guaranteed" results. Think about it: If there was such a thing as a quick, easy, guaranteed way to make lots of money, everyone would be doing it. In truth, it almost always takes time, hard work, and a bit of a risk to be successful in life.

Enlisting Help from the Feds

To file a complaint about a job offering or to get free information on a wide variety of consumer matters, you can go to the Federal Trade Commission's Web site at www.ftc.gov/bcp or call toll-free to 1-877-382-4357.

---

learned from and moved beyond any problems you have experienced in the past.

It is not easy to discuss these sorts of things with strangers, but it is an important part of learning how to conduct yourself as a young adult.

Deal honestly with dismissals. If you held a job and were fired, you are going to have to answer for it in one way or another. The best response is an honest one. If the company was forced to lay off employees because of economic conditions, say so. If you were terminated because it was not a good match for your capabilities, explain that in your résumé or your cover letter.

If you were fired for something you did wrong, discuss the situation with a guidance counselor or with a trusted adult and find a way to describe it simply and honestly. Most employers will respect your honesty; almost all will disqualify someone for dishonesty.

WHAT YOU NEED TO KNOW

▸ The Internet is a quick and easy way to look for job openings. But it is not the only place where jobs are advertised.

▸ Spend the time to construct an honest and detailed résumé before you post it online. Remember that employers may search the Internet to find out about applicants, and if they find conflicting information in your résumés in different places, they may drop you from consideration.

▸ Do not include information in a résumé, or supply it in an application, that is not necessary for the first step in a job application. For example, someone offering a job does not need to know your Social Security number or driver's license in order to consider you for a job, although these details are usually needed before employment is actually offered.

➤ If you plan to include references from previous jobs, contact your supervisors before you post or send the résumé to make sure they are willing to speak to new employers.

➤ Be cautious if someone advertising a job asks for personal information that the person does not need to know, at least in the early stages of interviewing. Some job postings are scams that are aimed at getting into your bank account.

➤ Think about the contents of your personal pages on the Internet. Is there anything posted there that will scare away an employer?

5

File-Sharing:
Free and Frightful

Digital recordings use numbers to describe sounds or dots on a video screen. They are stored as a "stream" of numbers in a computer, an iPod, or on a CD or DVD. Because they are just data, they can easily be moved around from place to place as a "file."

The portability of digital files is what allows us to buy music from an online store and download it to a player. It is also what allows us to watch a video or listen to music that comes over the Internet.

That's all very good. But where users can run into danger is if the files are copied and then shared or sold. There is nothing wrong with obtaining a file with your favorite song from an online music store or by buying it in the form of a CD in a shrink-wrapped box; that gives you the right to play the song as many times as you want, and you can bring it to school, to work, to the beach, or to a dance party.

But unless the artist who made the music or the recording company says otherwise, you are not legally permitted to make copies of the file to sell or even to give away. (Think of the book you have in your hands right now. You can read it. You can loan it to someone else. You can give it away, and you can even sell it to another person. But since it is protected by copyright law, you are not allowed to photocopy it or scan it into a computer and then publish it for sale as if its contents were yours.)

The same story applies to software you might buy for your computer. What you are purchasing is the right to install it and use it, but not to make copies and go into business on your own.

Books, music, videos, and patents are all considered intellectual property, and it seems that the easier it becomes to make copies of something, the harder it is for some people to understand why it is wrong to do so. Remember that artists or programmers have the right to make money from their inspiration just as a farmer has the right to earn a living from raising and selling chickens.

THE DANGERS OF FILE-SHARING

Enough about the moral and legal issues involved with making copies of digital files. There is more to it than just being fair.

The Internet and local networks have become the home for a number of "sharing" sites. One type is called peer-to-peer or P2P. The idea is that a group of individuals agree to share the files that are on their computers with one another. One of the first and most successful was Napster, which began in dorm rooms at Northeastern University in 1999.

Why are P2P sites dangerous? First, once they figured out what was going on, the owners of the copyrights for music, video, and software showed themselves to be quite aggressive in going after people who were giving away (or worse, selling) their product without permission. Napster was shut down by court order in 2001. (The Napster that is now in business is a different operation, selling legal copies of music under agreement with record companies.)

The second danger is that nasty people quickly figured out that a P2P network was a great way to spread viruses and other malware. All they had to do was insert their code into a music or video or other digital file and set it free.

The third danger involves the way some of the P2P networks were set up. Because the organizers were trying to avoid getting into legal trouble by actually storing and transmitting files, instead all of the files being shared remained on the computers of their members. All that the P2P organizers were posting online was an index of available songs, videos, or other files. If you saw something you wanted, you sent a request and a copy was taken off someone's personal machine and sent to you.

Think about that arrangement. As a member of a file-sharing group, you are basically opening the Internet door to your computer and telling the world to come on in. It did not take much effort for hackers to find ways to use P2P networks to harvest personal information about users—bank accounts, credit cards, and that sort of thing—or to send out viruses.

Keyloggers

One of the nastiest forms of spyware is something called a "keylogger." This little program, which can sneak in as part of something you download from a file-sharing program or arrive from an infected Web site, can keep records of everything you type from the keyboard and send that information to someone who hopes to find out your log-in names and passwords. Some of the latest versions even take snapshots of your screen and send them along.

HOW TO PROTECT YOURSELF

If you do choose to use a P2P network, there are some things you can do to try to protect yourself.

1. Install a high-quality Internet security program. Then be sure to keep it current with updates. And conduct regular scans of your system, looking for viruses and other malware that might come in with files you download or be planted by other users of the network.

2. Take great care in installing file-sharing software. Pay attention to the settings for the "shared" folder that you intend to use; be sure that it contains only files that are meant to be available on the network. If the P2P software has differing levels of security, be sure you understand the settings and choose the one that is as tight as possible; you want to do everything you can to limit others on the P2P network from going anywhere on your system except the folder you choose to open to them.

3. Be aware that some P2P networks make their money by running ads on your computer when you use their service. As part of the agreement to install the software, you may be giving them permission to install a form of adware.

4. Unless you have a very good reason to do so, set up your P2P software so that your computer is not connected to the network all the time. Be sure you understand how the service operates; some file-sharing networks automatically

load every time you turn on your machine and may be active in the background even if you are not using the network yourself.

5. Run an individual scan on any downloaded file before you first play it or use it. Most antivirus programs allow you to examine a specific file.

6. If your computer begins to show odd behavior—lost files, renamed files, crashes, or slowdowns—disconnect the machine from the Internet and run an antivirus and adware scan using your security software. If it detects problems related to the P2P network, you should consider uninstalling the file-sharing program.

Purposeful Spyware

Whether you like it or not, there are certain situations in which someone else may purposely put a keylogger or other form of spyware on your machine to keep an eye on you.

As a minor, your parents do have the right (and the responsibility) to protect you. There are a number of software programs that promise parents the ability to check up on which Web sites their children have visited or to make records of e-mails and instant messages.

If you think this sort of program might be on your system, you may be able to find it with an antivirus or antispyware utility, but remember that your parents may be alerted if you remove the program they installed. Instead, have an honest conversation with your parents. Ask them if they put the program on your machine, and if so, why. And then ask what you can do to earn their trust—and the removal of the spyware.

There are other places where it is perfectly legal for someone to watch every move you make: schools, libraries, and businesses. Schools and libraries may have filter programs that not only block access to certain types of sites but also alert someone of what you are doing.

If you get a job at a store or an office and have access to a computer, don't think that anything you do on the machine is private. An employer has the right to read all e-mail, keep copies of all instant messages, and make records of all Web sites you visit. (In fact, certain types of businesses are required by law to make and keep these records.)

7. Remember that you don't even have to be running a P2P program to pick up a virus. If a friend gives you a music or video file or a program downloaded through a P2P, a virus or adware may be embedded in the file.

8. Finally, even with all of these protections, if you use file-sharing networks, you should be careful about what sort of information you store on your computer. Avoid listing credit card numbers and bank accounts, and don't create a file that lists all of your user names and passwords. If you have any personal writing or photographs that you would not want strangers to read or see, don't store them on a computer that will be made a part of a P2P network. Then

How do you know your machine is infected?

Because your computer is a computer, it is sometimes capable of figuring out for itself that something has gone wrong because of malware. Look for warning messages from your operating system.

Any current antivirus or computer security program will also detect most infections. Depending on how you have set them up, they may just notify you of a problem and ask you what you want to do, or the program may just go right ahead and fix the problem.

If you don't get a warning but still suspect something odd is going on, here are some things to look for: new icons on your desktop, new favorites in your Internet browser (especially ones that seem to want to take you to places you have not visited and would not want to explore), and new toolbars. If you see any of these, close down any programs that are running—word processors, browsers, music players—and tell your antivirus or security program to run a manual scan of your computer. This may take a few hours.

If you remove adware or spyware that came along as part of a file-sharing program, you may find that you are no longer able to use that program. Think about it: The makers of the program are insisting that you allow them to spy on you or to clutter up your machine with adware and other junk.

make sure you make regular backup copies of all of your important files and store them away from your computer—on a CD or DVD, a flash memory key, or a removable hard drive; this way, if your computer becomes unusable, you still have recent versions of your files.

ANATOMY OF A FILE-SHARING FOUL-UP

Among the specific file-sharing programs that may cause the most problems are LimeWire, BitTorrent, Kazaa, and WinMX. Remember: Even though the company, group, or individual that operates the file-sharing service may be completely honest and have the best of intentions, there is no guarantee that one of the users of their product won't try to mess up the playground for the rest of us.

Some of these companies promise their products are "spyware-free" and then load up your computer with adware, including programs that report back to somewhere on the Internet about what you're up to when you're using your machine. Just because they call it something else doesn't mean that it is not spyware.

Here's a short and simple explanation of how one of these programs, LimeWire, works. Instead of keeping a bunch of files on one large computer and letting users sign on to get at them, this service concentrates on linking together individual machines owned by users.

In many ways, it operates like Facebook or other social networking sites. When you allow your machine to become a place known to LimeWire, you also let it become known to the machines of your friends. And through your friends your machine finds other groups of friends. Like an electronic chain letter, it does not take many steps before your computer is known to hundreds of thousands of other people—most of them strangers.

Once your machine is on the network, it can then search through any shared directories it finds. If you are looking for a particular song, your computer will hunt from machine to machine in search of it.

Your little search, then, is stealing time from your machine and dozens, hundreds, or thousands of other machines. Then if it finds the file, it brings it back to you. If you're lucky, all you'll get is what you asked for. If you're not lucky, you'll get the music plus a virus.

WHAT YOU NEED TO KNOW

▸ The nature of digital files—an organized collection of 0s and 1s that a computer can reconstruct into music, video, words,

Browser Hijackers

When you use an Internet browser, it always starts at a particular home page: It could be a search engine such as google.com or a newspaper Web site or anything else you choose. (Consult the help screens for your browser to learn how to set your preferred or "default" home page.)

One form of malware makes an annoying change to your settings, substituting a different home page. Someone might be doing this as a prank, or there might be a more dangerous problem: redirecting your browser to go to a page where your computer might be exposed to viruses and other malware. (Just say no to any offers of downloads.)

If you have an up-to-date antivirus program on your computer, it should be able to warn you that someone is trying to reset your home page and allow you to block the change. Otherwise, use your browser to go to the Web site you want as your home page and reassign it to fix the problem.

In the worst case, the hijacker program may have messed up your Internet browser so badly that you will need to reinstall a fresh copy of the browser. That's the bad news; the good news is that browsers are free from sources, including Microsoft (Internet Explorer), Google (Chrome), Mozilla (Firefox), and other companies.

or a program that can allow your machine to perform certain tasks—also makes them easy to copy.

- The fact that you can make a copy of a digital file does not mean you have the right to give (or sell) a copy to someone else. Most performances, literary works, and programs are copyrighted, and you may be violating the law.
- Because files are coming from other peoples' computers, you cannot know if they are infected with viruses, spyware, or other malware. A capable and up-to-date antivirus program should protect you from most threats, but some problems may not be obvious until you try to use the file, and some malware may get past firewalls and antivirus programs.

6

E-mail Scams and Internet Fraud

Dear Stranger: Have I got a deal for you!

Has anyone ever come up to you on the street and offered you a free car, or a suitcase full of money, or an all-expenses paid trip to Paris? If they did, wouldn't you be very, very suspicious?

What if the next thing this person said was, "Oh, and by the way, before I give you this free gift I need you to give me a few hundred dollars for expenses and fees, and I also need your bank account number, your credit card number, and all of your online passwords." You would likely walk away quickly.

Of course, this sort of thing does not happen on the street. If it did, the police would be very busy making arrests for fraud.

In the modern digital world, crooks can reach out and try to steal your wallet from anywhere. By doing it from some of the more obscure corners of the planet, they can make it hard or even impossible for the police in your town, the FBI, or local courts to find them or put them in jail.

READING YOUR MAIL

The first thing to do is to take the time to read messages carefully before you even think about responding to them. In most cases, it should take only a few seconds to determine that someone is trying to scam you.

Start with this general set of rules:

1. If an offer sounds too good to be true, it almost always is not true.
2. A serious offer of a prize or notification of an award from a government or an attorney will usually come in the form of a personally addressed letter, together with full details about the sender.
3. If something is "free," then it should not cost you money to get it.

If that's not what you're reading, stop. Do not reply. Do not forward the scam to a friend. Delete.

Never forget that criminals are smart, in a stupid kind of way. On the Internet, they don't need a gun. Instead, they're looking for some way to fool people into giving them money or information, or unlocking the online door to bank accounts and credit cards.

But you're smart too. When you are in cyberspace, you have the advantage of not having to deal with someone who is in your face. You can take the time to think about what you're being asked to do, and you can always hang up or disconnect. The more someone pushes you to act quickly or claims that this is a "one-time" offer, the more you should dig in your heels and slow down.

The rules for dealing with e-mail are the same as anywhere else online. Keep your personal information and your banking accounts to

Don't Return to Sender

Why should you not reply to a scammer? Most scams are sent out to huge lists of e-mail addresses gathered from many sources; the crooks are hoping that maybe one in a few hundred thousand of the people who get their message will bite at the hook.

If you reply to the message, you are telling scammers that you exist. And you are practically begging them to come back at you with a tsunami of new attempts to convince you to play along with their scheme. If they can figure out your phone number or your street address, they may try to reach you in other ways.

Remember that they are trying to steal from you. Why would you expect them to politely remove your name from their list?

yourself until you are certain you are dealing with a company you can trust. Never buy anything or provide information to a company or a person unless you are able to get and check full details about name, location, and telephone number.

If you do decide to go ahead and make a purchase, read all of the guarantees and be sure you understand whether you will have the right to return something if you decide you don't want to keep it. Will you have to pay for shipping in both directions? Are there "restocking" fees for returns?

Make a copy of the policies as you see them at the time of purchase. Print them out or make an electronic screen capture.

Then remember that the best way to pay for something—once you have made a good effort to determine if the seller is for real—is to use a credit card or certain types of debit cards that are backed by one of the credit card companies. (For example, these debit cards would have the logo of Visa or Mastercard on them.) Using a credit card gives you certain rights, protected by federal law, that allow you to dispute charges for purchases or services that are not delivered, are not as promised, or that are the result of fraud.

CROSS-BORDER E-MAIL SCAMS

In old westerns and crime movies, the bad guys always had a not-so-secret strategy to escape the law. They would "run for the border." Sheriff's deputies on horses or the police in their squad cars chase them at full speed right up to the sign that said "border," and then they stop and watch the bandits get away . . . until next time.

Free, After You Pay

What is it about "free" that they don't understand? That's a proper question you should ask yourself any time someone offers you "free" money or merchandise and then tries to convince you that all you need to do is pay a service charge or a finder's fee or whatever the particular scam is they are trying to pull. Every once in a lifetime, you may actually win a prize. Accept it with thanks and enjoy it. But don't pay for it.

Today, that sort of an escape route doesn't really work for most crimes. The U.S. government has agreements with most countries around the world that allows the arrest and prosecution of people who try to run away; the same applies among all of the states.

But in the modern Internet world, things have gotten sticky when someone attempts or actually commits a crime from outside the United States against an American citizen. (And it is not just limited to Americans who may be victimized by foreigners.)

As a consumer, you should be very careful about any offer you receive from someone outside of your home country. Some may be legitimate, but many are scams.

NIGERIAN SCAMS

There are many fine and honest citizens in Nigeria who are likely very unhappy about the fact that their country's name has become attached to an entire class of scam artists.

In recent years, nearly every one with an e-mail account has received at least one of several dozen variations of an appeal or a scheme that includes a reference to Nigeria. There's another name some law-enforcement agencies use for these scams: They may call them 4-1-9 frauds. That name comes from the Nigerian law that is supposed to make them illegal. But there are also thousands of Internet crooks who have absolutely no connection with the country, which has the largest population in all of Africa.

Here's the general outline of a Nigerian scam:

1. You receive an e-mail from a banker, secretary, social worker, lawyer, or a bureaucrat. They may call themselves a doctor, a minister, a barrister (an English term for lawyer), or other title.
2. Somehow the sender has gotten your e-mail address—even though the letter you receive may not have your name on it.
3. A terrible thing has happened, or a big mistake has been made. Someone made a deposit of cash in a bank and then was killed by terrorists. Or a woman left a suitcase of money with a lawyer and then died in a car crash. Perhaps a charity has given millions as a gift but for some reason cannot deposit the cash in a bank. Or someone says he is a bureaucrat and writes to tell you he has found millions of unspent dollars in an account that everyone in the government has forgotten about.

4. In every case, there seem to be no relatives or other people who are entitled to the money. But there are all sorts of crooked politicians and thieves (imagine that?) trying to take away the money.

5. For some reason, they think you can be trusted to help them, even though you've never heard of them and they don't know anything about you. And if you were to look closely at the e-mail itself—anyone who has experience with computer software should be able to help you examine the "properties" of the message—you would see that the e-mail was sent to dozens or hundreds of people.

6. They would like to send you the money so you can deposit it and keep a portion of it as your reward before sending the rest back to them. Or they would like you to send them some money so that they can send you the money. Or they would like you to give them all of the details of your bank accounts so they can put the money in there and later you can send them their share.

It all sounds very silly, doesn't it? Why would a complete stranger ask you to share in a fortune, and why would you give personal or financial information to someone who approaches you out of the blue?

And yet, every day people fall for this scam. There is just enough detail in the e-mails to make some people think the story is true. Unfortunately, there are some people who turn off their brains when someone offers what seems to be quick and easy riches.

Every year hundreds and perhaps thousands of people send money or information to one of these scammers. A handful have even been convinced to travel to a foreign nation to meet in person with the people involved; according to the U.S. State Department, some have been threatened, beaten, and even murdered.

A SCAM WITHIN A SCAM

The crooks have been at this game for many years, always trying to find new ways to fool people. One of the latest wrinkles is an attempt to give you an almost believable reason to accept their unbelievable offer.

An actual e-mail scam received by the author of this book started out with the same sort of ridiculous claim about a total stranger—in Nigeria, surprise surprise—who had decided to give to him no less than $60 million in his will.

"This may sound strange and unbelievable to you, but it is real and true," the e-mail continued. "Being a widely traveled man, he must

Advice from Federal Crime-fighters

The Federal Trade Commission and other major American government agencies are trying to educate people not to respond. If you receive an e-mail from Nigeria or any other country with this sort of appeal, do not respond to it. Instead, forward it to the FTC at spam@uce.gov

Other federal agencies that are involved in fighting this type of crime include the U.S. Secret Service and the U.S. Postal Service's postal inspectors.

If you have actually lost money in one of these schemes, you may be able to get help—or at least prevent others from becoming victims—by contacting the nearest office of the U.S. Secret Service. You can find the number in your phone book, through a Web search, or by calling your local police department.

have been in contact with you in the past or simply you were nominated to him by one of his numerous friends abroad who wished you good. According to him this money is to support your humanitarian activities and to help the poor and the needy in our society."

Another variation on a scam within a scam is to contact someone by e-mail with a pitch that talks about the fact that *some people* out there are crooked—but not the sender of this particular ripoff.

Aside from the fact that the following letter makes very little sense if you read it carefully, you've got to give the crooks a bit of credit for creativity. Here's the exact text of a scam that apologizes for impersonators claiming to be attorneys or officials and then goes on to make the same sort of pitch.

FROM: PROF. CHUKWUMA C. SOLUDO
CENTRAL BANK OF NIGERIA
P.M.B.33245 KARARINPIGA RANUBA
Executive Governor (CBN)

Attn: Beneficiary,

Following series of petitions and complaints received from the International Monetary Funds (IMF) about Nigerians on your behalf and based on our own investigation on foreign payment matters, we are glad to inform you that we are aware of the illegal contact/dealing made to you by some impersonators claiming to be Attorneys, Bank Officials and Directors of different Offices in the Nigerian Government.

Recently, we received a petition that you spent so much money on several occasion to these people. You are therefore advised to stop dealing with these people as they are trying to divert your funds from the records of outstanding CONTRACTORS / INHERITANCE due for payment with the Federal Government of Nigeria, your name / company was discovered as next on the list of the outstanding contractors/Inheritors who have not received their payments.

I wish to inform you that your payment is being processed and will be released to you as soon as you respond to this letter. Also note that from my record and the file submitted to my office by the Office of the United Nation Monitoring Unit, London your outstanding contract / inheritance payment is Twelve Million, Five Hundred Thousand United States Dollars (US$12,500,000.00). But it has been approved by the Federal Government of Nigerian in collaboration with the United Nation's Monitoring Unit, London, to pay you the sum of Ten Million United States Dollars (US$10,000,000.00) for this fourth quarter payments of this fiscal year. And hopeful to pay the remaining balance within first quarter of next year.

Therefore, prior to this payment arrangement, you are hereby requested to re-confirm to this office the following information:

1) Your full names and address.................
2) Phone, fax and mobile #......................
3) Ocupation, position and address..........
4) Profession,sex,age and marital status.........
5) Working Id/Int'l passport copy...............

As soon as the above stated informations are received, your payment will be made to you in a Certified Bank Draft or transferred to your nominated Bank account through international Telegraphic Transfer (TT) directly from Central Bank of Nigeria. And thereafter, a copy of the transfer slip will be given to you for you're up taking to your Bank for confirmation.

Note that the earlier you respond to this mail, the better for immediate transfer of your over due contract funds to your nominated bank account.

Thanks, and we regret any inconveniences this might have caused you.

Regards,

Prof. Chukwuma C. Soludo
Executive Governor,
Central Bank of Nigeria (CBN)

CONGRATULATIONS! YOU'VE WON THE LOTTERY

Don't jump up and down too much. First, it is against United States law for a citizen to buy a foreign lottery ticket by mail or by electronic purchase, which would be the only ways you would likely pay for your ticket. Second, although there are lotteries in many parts of the world, most have rules that make it difficult or impossible for foreigners to collect. Third, just for the record, the chances of winning any major lottery (including lotteries that may be run by the state where you live) are about the same as you being hit by a meteor in your

---

Your Government Wants to Help

You can send your criminal spam to the Federal Trade Commission for investigation by using the "forward" button on your e-mail account and using this address: spam@uce.gov

International Consumer Protection and Enforcement Network. www.econsumer.gov

FTC identity theft Web site. www.ftc.gov/idtheft

Secret Service field offices. www.secretservice.gov/field_offices. shtml

U.S. Department of State advisories. www.state.gov/www/regions/ africa/naffpub.pdf

Competition Bureau (Canada). www.competitionbureau.gc.ca

Hello, Sucker

How'd you like to officially be known as a "sucker"? The way most Internet con artists work is that they send their messages to any and every e-mail address they can find. If one in a million bites at an offer, they're happy to steal the money. And then the e-mail address and other information from the victim goes onto a "sucker list" that will be used again and again ... and often is sold or traded from one crook to another. That's a club you really do not want to join.

backyard while you are reading this book and while you are hopping up and down on your left leg while waving your right hand in the air. In other words, not very likely. And the chances of winning if you never even entered the lottery? That would be zero.

Most of these scams are not at all interested in trying to sell you a ticket—even if it was legal. And they're certainly not going to pay you hundreds of thousands or millions of dollars for a lottery you never entered. Instead, what they're likely to try and do is find ways to convince you to pay service charges, bank transaction charges, shipping charges, or whatever phony line they can offer. Others will tell you they need your bank account numbers and passwords so they can transfer your winnings; they are, of course, hoping to suck your money out instead.

Here's another type of e-mail scam: a super-secret lottery that you don't even have to enter in order to win. Just for the record, the United Nations does not run lotteries, and there is no such thing as a global tax-free lottery,

Dear Lucky Winner:

Congratulations! You have won $15 million in the biannual top-secret United Nations Global Tax-Free Lottery! Yes, we know you've never heard of this lottery; that's why it's called top-secret. And of course, we're sure you're saying, "I never bought a ticket in the UNGTFL, so how could I win?" That's the beauty of this wonderful giveaway: It's so secret that other people enter your name for you.

Now, all you have to do to claim your $15 million is to tell us where you want the money deposited. We'll need your bank account number, your ATM PIN, your credit card number, and (of course) your user name and your password. Oh, and your Social Security number and your address so that we can make sure that all the forms are filled out properly.

Do not tell anyone about this great reward you have received or else you will have to pay taxes and bank fees and you will become ineligible for future United Nations awards.

Sounds like an honest story and a reasonable request, right? Not!

If you can't see through the gigantic holes in that message, go out and buy a bottle of eye drops for yourself and glass cleaner for your computer screen.

THE MISADDRESSED PACKAGE SCAM

You're not expecting a package. There is no reason you know of why someone would be sending you an $850,000 bank draft, and the letter is written with words and phrases that seem lost in translation from some strange language. But someone out there is going to fall for this con. Let's call it the misaddressed package scam.

Here's an actual e-mail that arrived in the author's mailbox while he was writing this book. It is reproduced here exactly as it was received, except for changed e-mail addresses and phone numbers.

> From: Fedex Courier Service
> I have a new email address!
> You can now email me at: nocompany1234@yahoo.in
>
> Compliment of the day,did you assigned Mrs. Janet White.To make the claim or collection of your parcel which contains an international bank draft worth $850,000.00 dollars,on your behalf?Furthermore,if you are not aware, please quickly notify us and if you want the continuity of the shipment,you have to re-send to us your informations mention below: 1.Name 2.Address3.Telephone To avoid any further mistake or error. The above required information will help and enable us re-package and create a new tracking number for you,since your parcel has been sent back to our office. Moreover, you should be expecting your parcel within two(2) days that 48 hours once we receive your payment. CallMe on:Phone: + 234-702XXXXXXXForward your response urgently to: raga233@post.roRegardsMr.MikeBrownPhone: + 234-702XXXXXXX

This one, I hope, is a lot more obviously fake than some other scams you may have seen. There are dozens of clues, including the very odd spacing used between words and the unusual phrases. ("Compliment of the day" to you too.)

It starts trying to fool you into thinking it is coming from a real brand-name delivery service, "Fedex Courier Service." Only, that is not the proper name or styling; the company is called FedEx Corporation, something you could find out very easily by typing "Fedex" into a search engine on the Internet.

But then the message suddenly changes from a communication that claims to be from a company to an email that was sent by an individual. "I have a new e mail address," it begins. That's odd. Even stranger, the e-mail address is not one at Federal Express but instead uses a public e-mail service through Yahoo (others like this include Gmail or services offered by Internet providers like AOL, cable television companies, or telephone companies.)

Read on, and things get even weirder. The e-mail address is at yahoo.in, which means it was registered in India. Why would a notification to you about a package meant to be delivered to you by FedEx come from an e-mail address in India?

And then Mr. Mike Brown (which sounds like an odd name for someone with an e-mail address in India) provides a telephone number for you to call. It begins with +234, which tells you that it is an international call. If you were to go to your search engine and enter "Country Code 234," you would learn that 234 is used for Nigeria.

Doing Your Own Detective Work

Use the power of the Internet to check on any company you are considering doing business with. From a search engine, enter the company's name; skip the "official" Web site for the company and look for entries by happy or unhappy customers with reports about how they were treated.

Some people do the same thing when they get a phone call from someone they don't know. They make a note of the telephone number, then enter it into a search engine. More often than not, the result for the unknown phone number is page after page of complaints about telemarketers or even thieves. Then the individual can add that number to their list of "blocked" callers.

Finally, just to make things even more interesting, Mr. Brown also provides an e-mail address for you to "forward your response urgently to," and it is a different one from the address at the top of the e-mail. This one is at another public e-mail service, "post.ro," which means (you can check this through a Web search) that the address is in Romania in eastern Europe.

All of these weird and strange bits of information should be enough to convince you to ignore—and delete from your system—this sort of message without even spending the time to wade through the curious message. Do you really expect someone you don't know, who maybe lives in India, Nigeria, or Romania, or possibly somewhere else, to have a check for you for $850,000 that you didn't know about?

How Bad Can It Get?

In November 2008, a woman in Oregon told police and reporters that she had lost $400,000 to scammers in Nigeria who convinced her that she could receive $20.5 million in return.

The particular pitch she fell for, reported by the Associated Press and KATU-TV, included the name of a long-lost relative. Whether the crooks had accidentally come up with a name she recognized or whether they had found the name by doing a little searching on the Internet was not known.

The letters eventually included realistic-looking bank documents from Nigeria and the United Nations, and forged letters that appeared to be from President George W. Bush, the director of the FBI, and the president of Nigeria. The woman was told to keep the story secret so that "terrorists" would not get their hands on the money.

But the name of the relative was what convinced her to send money, she said. "That's what got me to believe it," she told reporters. "So, why wouldn't you send over $100?"

The hundred dollars became several hundred dollars, and then eventually nearly all of her retirement savings and a mortgage on her house. When her family and bank officials tried to convince her that it was a scam and begged her to stop, she said she became obsessed with getting paid what she was promised.

PYRAMID SCAMS

Have you ever gotten one of those chain letters that promises you immense riches for what seems like little or no risk? There are many different types of this sort of appeal, and over time none of them results in a happy ending.

Here's one example: "How would you like to receive hundreds of thousands of dollars in the mail from complete strangers? All you have to do is send $10 to the three names at the top of the list. Then take the #1 person's name off the list and put your name on the bottom and send this letter to 10 of your friends. Within weeks, your name will be at the top of the list and the money will start rolling in! What do you have to lose?"

Well, you have $30 and maybe 10 of your friends to lose. And the chances of thousands of dollars coming your way are pretty slim.

A chain letter is a version of something called a "pyramid scheme," and it amounts to a form of gambling. There's also a financial scam that is similar, called a "Ponzi scheme."

If you receive any of these appeals by e-mail or through a Web site, think about the way this works: Someone who is at the top of the chain will probably find more than a few investors who will send money. Maybe one or two of the 10 friends you send the letter to will keep the chain unbroken. But the chances are pretty good that your name will drop off the list, or the list will stop, long before it has gone through as many as 10 waves of mailings.

Do the math: If you send out 10 letters, and each of your friends follows instructions and sends out 10 letters, the letter has now been duplicated and mailed 110 times. The next wave would have 100 people sending out 1,000 letters, and on and on. If everyone cooperates, at the end of 10 cycles there would be 10 billion people ready to send you $10 each. Slight problem there: The population of entire planet is about 7 billion. Other more significant problem: Most people throw away or ignore e-mail chain letters.

The only people who make money—usually not all that much—from a chain letter scheme are the first few people involved in starting the scam. They put their name at the top and hope to get as many people as they can to start the ball rolling.

Before you think this is a great way to start a business, the U.S. Postal Service considers this sort of appeal as an illegal gambling scheme, and there are also laws and regulations that apply to online operations. (One loophole: online individuals or groups who operate from foreign countries. But that alone ought to prove that these schemes are scams.)

Some people try to play on your emotions and fears by promising to cure cancer or feed the hungry if you keep the chain alive—or to curse you and your family for 10 generations if you let the chain break. If you want to make a contribution to a legitimate charity, please do so. But don't let someone pick your pocket with a chain letter.

MULTILEVEL MARKETING

A variation of the pyramid schemes is called multilevel marketing operations. Some of these are legal and some illegal. Be sure to involve a trusted adult if you are considering getting involved with one.

The basic way MLMs work is like this: You are offered the "opportunity" to distribute or sell some wonderful product or service. You'll have to put up some money to become a distributor, and then you can sell to your friends, family, and strangers. That's the first level.

The real money—or so they claim—comes if you are successful in selling not the product but more distributorships. In other words, you will try to get friends, family, and strangers to buy the same "opportunity" that got you involved. In this second level, you are promised a commission (a percentage of the value) on the sales from every other distributor you recruit, plus a smaller commission from every distributor your distributors recruit, and so on.

Again, think about the math. In theory, the person at the top of this pyramid stands to make money from dozens or hundreds or thousands of people who buy into the MLM scheme. The further down the chain you are, the smaller your cut.

But here is where some MLMs run into trouble. The first problem arises with legitimate companies selling a real product; sooner or later there are so many little slices of the profit going to so many levels of the pyramid that the product cannot possibly be sold at a profit.

The other kind of problem arises when an MLM is an out-and-out fraud. Some companies exist only to sell distributorships and have no real product or service. The people involved hope to keep money by selling more and more distributorships and passing along commissions without ever offering a product to the public.

If you receive an e-mail or find yourself being offered a plan like this at a Web site, you may want to ask a knowledgeable and trusted adult for help in examining the offer. You can call or contact the Better Business Bureau or your state's attorney general office and ask about the plan.

Some of these MLM schemes may be legal and well intentioned, but many are not. And none of them offer you "free money for no work."

PONZI SCHEMES

The type of financial pyramid known as a Ponzi scheme was named after Charles Ponzi, an immigrant who did not invent the scam but is credited with conducting the first major use of it in the United States in 1903.

In the simplest terms, a Ponzi scheme is a way to make some investors a lot of money by paying them out of new money that comes in from new investors. Here's an example: If someone told you, "Give me $100 today and I'll pay you $110 tomorrow," you might think that was a pretty good deal. Then tomorrow, that same person would make the same offer to someone else and use part of that second $100 to pay you your profit. (Even better: If this person can convince you to reinvest your "profits," he or she doesn't have to come up with money to pay you now.)

In theory, that process can work as long as you keep getting more and more new investments to pay off earlier investors. But eventually—like a pyramid scheme or a chain letter—you'll reach a point where you'll need a huge amount of fresh money each time the cycle repeats. If one day you cannot find enough investors, the pyramid will collapse.

The main difference from a multilevel marketing scheme is that for a Ponzi scheme there is one person or one company at the hub of the process instead of layer upon layer of sellers and resellers. Some versions of Ponzi schemes claim to involve some sort of special investment—in gold or diamonds or an unusual type of stock or bond—while others just claim they have some sort of magic that allows them to pay you back much more than you invest.

If this sounds too silly to work, consider that in late 2008, a New York man, Bernie Madoff, and the investment company he ran were revealed to have run what may have been the largest Ponzi scheme ever known. Something like $50 billion in investments may have been lost, wiping out individuals, companies, and charities around the world.

WHAT YOU NEED TO KNOW

▸ You've heard this before, but it's should be the first thing you think of when you receive an astounding offer in your e-mail: If it sounds too good to be true, it almost certainly is.

▸ There is almost no chance that someone you have never met is going to pick your name out of a hat and send you a fortune. And if that very, very remote chance were to happen, why would this stranger ask you to send money?

➤ An entire class of Internet thieves has its roots in places such as Nigeria and eastern Europe. I'm not saying that everyone in those places is a crook, but if you see even the slightest hint that an e-mail offer comes from far-off places like these, you should be very suspicious about what you read.

➤ A chain letter, pyramid scam, or a Ponzi scheme may seem to make sense when you look at it on a small-scale level. But in order for any of them to deliver their promise of huge profits for a small investment, they require the cooperation of hundreds, thousands, or millions of people; they almost never work for very long.

➤ Multilevel marketing schemes are based on the sale of the right to sell a product. Participants take a small profit from the sales made by those they recruit. The more people involved the more slices of profit are taken . . . and the more likely the entire enterprise will fail.

➤ Ponzi schemes are frauds. They pay yesterday's investors with new money that comes in today. Eventually, the scheme collapses from its own weight or because not enough new money can be found.

7

Internet Drugstores

There are three reasons people buy prescription drugs over the Internet: in hopes of paying less than they would at a neighborhood drugstore; as an attempt to buy certain drugs without seeing a doctor to get a prescription; because they want to order certain types of medications in privacy.

Everyone wants to save money, especially in difficult times. And even though there are some Internet drugstores that are honest and safe, there are many more that are not. You could end up with phony drugs that will do nothing to help you, mislabeled or outdated drugs that could hurt you, or you could end up the victim of a crook who will simply steal your money and fade away into cyberspace.

Let's start with this very important rule: No one, not teens or adults, should use any prescription drug without visiting a doctor or a medical center first. The reason certain drugs are sold only by prescription is that the federal Food and Drug Administration and the drugmakers themselves have determined that a doctor should be involved in monitoring their use.

(It's not the purpose of this book to discuss abuse of illegal street drugs, including narcotics, but for the record: Can we all agree that they can ruin your health, land you in jail, and destroy your educational and career dreams?)

The second very important rule: Speak with a responsible adult before making any purchase of medications by yourself. If for some reason you don't want to discuss a private matter with your parents, you can ask your school nurse or your doctor for advice. Don't take chances with your health.

ORDERING LEGAL MEDICATIONS OVER THE INTERNET

There are a number of companies that will fill prescriptions from your doctor over the Internet. Some are online branches of major drugstore chains, and some are specialized operations that work with your health insurance company.

You can either send your prescription to the company by postal mail (you know, that ancient technology that uses an envelope and a stamp and takes a few days to get across town), or in some systems your doctor may be allowed to send a prescription by fax.

You take care of the payment by credit or debit card or by direct withdrawal from your bank account. The service then mails you the medications once it receives the prescription.

This sort of service works well if you take a prescription for a long period of time—for example, allergy pills or asthma inhalers. If your doctor wants you to immediately start taking an antibiotic because you have an infection, you're not going to want to wait a few days or a week for the medication to arrive.

GRAY-MARKET DRUGS

There are some real pharmacies in the United States, Canada, Mexico, and elsewhere around the world that require a doctor's prescription but offer major discounts on medications because they sell drugs that are imported from other countries. These are sometimes called "gray-market" products.

Many of the prescription drugs that you buy at your neighborhood pharmacy may actually have been manufactured in foreign countries. But they are made for major companies, pass American inspection, and almost always are exactly what your doctor has ordered. You do not have those same promises if you buy on the gray market.

BLACK-MARKET DRUGS

And then we come to the black market, the source of medications that are sold in e-mail spam you may receive or on Web sites you may visit. Some don't require a prescription at all, while others may offer to sell you a prescription from someone who is thousands of miles away and may or may not be a licensed doctor.

First question: Do you really think it is worth risking your health by purchasing something from someone who sends you spam? The drugs may be fake, they may be out of date, they may have not been properly stored, or they may be poorly manufactured or contaminated.

Second question: Are you willing to run the risk of federal legal problems because you are importing drugs improperly?

Third question: What possible protection do you expect to receive from your credit or debit card company or your bank if you place an order and are ripped off? In most situations, you will not get help for any purchase they consider illegal.

ROGUE WEB SITES

Some drug Web sites get around the requirement that you provide them with a doctor's prescription by arranging for an online or telephone "consultation" with a physician. You'll pay a fee, just as you would if you went to your own doctor, but obviously you will not receive a physical exam, any tests, or much of a review of your medical history.

According to industry reports, some of these sites require customers to fill out a "consultation" form that includes some history and symptoms; in a number of cases, the forms arrive with the "correct" answers already filled in or with a list of suggested answers. Either way, you are not protected from possible side effects or dangers to your health because of your own personal medical history.

No One Knew

In 2008, CBS News reported on research done at Columbia University that claimed 85 percent of Web sites selling drugs do not require a prescription. These included what are supposed to be tightly controlled drugs, including painkillers and tranquilizers; both of these classes of drugs can cause death or serious injury if abused.

Linda Surks, whose son Jason died because of an overdose of an anxiety medicine he purchased over the Internet from Mexico—without a prescription—said the situation was "despicable."

Speaking of her son, she said, "He was really a fabulous person who made a horrible mistake."

Finding a Certified Online Pharmacy

One way you can protect yourself when buying prescription drugs online is to use a site that has been certified by the National Association of Boards of Pharmacy. This group publishes a list of Verified Internet Pharmacy Practice Sites at www.nabp.net, as well as a long list of sites they do not recommend.

In addition to the NABP list, you may also find that your health insurance company can tell you which online sites it recommends. Call the customer service phone number on your insurance card for assistance.

WHAT YOU NEED TO KNOW

> ▸ Legitimate Internet drugstores can offer savings in cost and be more convenient than going to a neighborhood pharmacy. They require that you mail a prescription from your doctor, or have the prescription sent by fax from your doctor's office.

> ▸ Sites that offer to sell drugs without a prescription or those that offer to arrange for a doctor to write a prescription for you without meeting you or examining you present a real danger to your health or your wallet.

8

Finding That Special Someone

So you think that it might be fun—and safer—to meet someone online instead of waiting to find the Right One by chance. It certainly is safer to play the field when you are locked away in your house and the only connection between you and another person is the Internet. But what happens if you decide to take the next step and meet someone in person? If you've only exchanged messages or spoken on the phone, you really don't know all that much about the person.

Before you say, "He's sent me a picture" or "She sounds so nice," stop and think: How can you be sure that someone isn't trying to fool you? Anyone could send you a picture of another person and say it is him or her; the person could also hand the phone to someone else and ask that person to chat you up.

If you meet someone at a party or school or are introduced through friends, you can ask a few questions. "What do you know about J. B.? Is everything cool? Here's what I was told; is any of it true?"

Of course, not everyone who participates in online dating services or meets people in chat rooms is dangerous or weird or in any other way different from someone you might meet first in person. The Internet is just another form of communication. But do remember: Just as there are creeps you might meet on the street, there are also creeps who lurk online.

When it comes to online introductions or flirting or dating, here's the bottom line: Be careful when you open yourself up to meet with anyone for a date or even a casual get-together. Because you have become acquainted with someone over the Internet instead of meeting him or her in person, you should be even more cautious.

ONLINE DATING AND FLIRTING SITES

There are more than a dozen major online matchmaking and dating sites on the Internet and hundreds of other small or informal sites. Some of the places are very well organized and provide many layers of security to users, including attempts at screening the ages and backgrounds of everyone who signs up. Others are little more than online bulletin boards with little or no supervision.

Craigslist, for example, has "personal ads" in many regions around the country. To read them or to post one of your own, all you need to do is click on a button agreeing to the following:

> ▸ You are at least 18 years old.
> ▸ You understand that the ads may include "adult" content.
> ▸ You agree to release Craigslist from any liability (that means you promise not to sue them) for anything that might happen to you as a result of using their site.

Users agree to notify others or law-enforcement authorities if they see something illegal. But basically, you're on your own at Craigslist. No one actually checks to see if you are 18 years old or that the name you give is your real one or that any other information you list is correct.

Craigslist is just one example of a nearly unsupervised site. There are many local listings that operate with similar rules or lack of rules.

Some sites announce their policies but clearly leave it to others to police users. For example, at AOL Personals, the listings are topped by the following advisory: "Note: This is an advice board for those 18 years old and over."

TEEN DATING SITES

In between the "wild west" of the unsupervised dating sites and the "adults-only" matchmaking services are places like eCRUSH.com, which are aimed specifically at teens and includes some good intentions when it comes to user safety.

An old-timer in the business, eCRUSH was founded in 1999; it was bought by Hearst Magazines in 2007. Most of its features are free, with the company earning its profits from advertising. According to eCRUSH, the site is visited by more than 1.5 million people each month, nearly all of them 13 to 19 years old.

The eCRUSH site is intended to allow you to find out if someone you like feels the same about you, without—at first—revealing who you are. Another site, eSPIN-the-Bottle, is a version of an online matchmaking service aimed at teens. All submissions from young users are screened to make sure they do not contain any information that would allow someone to identify them or find them; e-mail addresses or chat room names are released only when two people agree to exchange information with each other.

The company tells users, "In real life, you would never give private information to a stranger. Play by the same rules online."

Here is part of eCRUSH's safety policies:

> No personally identifiable info is allowed in your profile. If you're here to try to share that kind of information, you're on the wrong site.
> We screen all photos before other users can see them, and we screen public comments from users under 18.
> We never, ever allow adults to contact minors, and vice versa.
> If you do see something inappropriate (or fake, or gross), we've provided a "report this photo" link under all user photos.
> Before two users can send mail, they have to be mutual matches (by checking out each other's profiles and agreeing to be connected) which means you won't get gross, unsolicited mail from creeps.

ONLINE DATING SAFETY TIPS

Among the leaders in online matchmaking and dating sites are eHarmony and match.com. Although most online dating sites are aimed at older users—at least 18 years old—it is almost impossible to keep out young people who might fudge a bit about their birthday. The safety tips these sites offer their users are important for people of all ages.

Here are some recommendations drawn from eHarmony, match. com, and other online dating sites, and from good old common sense:

1. If something doesn't feel right, trust your instincts. If you're a 15-year-old girl, you have a pretty good idea what it's like to talk to a boy at your school; if someone sounds like they are trying too hard to act like someone your age, they just might be trying to fool you.

2. If someone sounds too good to be true, they might be just that—not true. Think about the friends you do have. The good ones are those who sometimes agree with you, sometimes disagree, but are always on your side. You should be suspicious of someone who thinks everything you say and do is so smart or so funny or so cool. Your best friends probably are not shy about bringing you down a notch; people trying to take advantage of you, though, might not quarrel with you if you told them the moon was made of cheese.

3. For the same reasons, beware of someone who tries to make himself or herself seem like the greatest person on the planet. The person may be trying too hard to impress you, which might be quite harmless, or the person may be completely making up his or her story. And keep your radar on for someone who gives very vague answers to specific questions.

4. Watch out for people who want to zoom from casual friend to best buddy to lover as if they were in a race. Always proceed on the pace that feels most comfortable for you; never allow yourself to be pressured.

5. If someone you know only casually asks you for money or for some kind of assistance in a financial transaction like depositing a check and sending you the money, don't give it a second thought. Why would someone be doing that? There are no good reasons, only scams. Contact eHarmony or another dating service if you are using it, or ask an adult to assist you in reporting an attempt at fraud.

6. Exercise the same sort of caution if someone you scarcely know suddenly seeks your assistance in dealing with a highly personal crisis. The person may tell you it's about a medical crisis or a problem with the police, but it's almost always about the money . . . yours, if you fall for it.

7. If eHarmony closes someone's account because the activities are suspicious or they receive reports of inappropriate behavior, you may be notified by e-mail and advised to stop communicating with that person. The company recommends members to read carefully any official e-mails it sends.

SOMEBODY CALL SECURITY

Most online dating services do not perform criminal or financial background checks on the people who use their sites other than to make sure that the membership fees are paid regularly.

Most services merely ask their members to provide information such as their name, address, phone number, and sometimes further identification like driver's license number or place of employment; they do not verify that the information is correct.

The eHarmony site offers users the chance to add a bit more substance to their listing through the use of a service called RelyID, which matches names against a database of public information, including criminal records, education graduation information, employment records, and certain types of certification or licensing made by organizations or government agencies.

Services like RelyID are better than having no checks done at all, but keep in mind a few things:

1. Not all people who commit crimes are arrested or put on trial.
2. There is no national registry of persons convicted of crimes; not every state, city, and town reports every court proceeding.
3. Some convictions, including many involving young persons, are removed from records or sealed from view.
4. If a person files for bankruptcy or is sued, that information is usually available as a public record. But if someone tells you he is a millionaire with a yacht, a background check may or may not tell you if that is true or false.
5. If someone successfully creates an alias—a name and other information that is different from the birth name—the person may be able to fool some background checks. This is something that is becoming harder to do as employers and banks ask to see proof of identity, but a determined person can often find a way to assume a new name, at least for a while.
6. Someone could assume the identity of someone else and completely fool most background checking services. For example, if somebody knew your name, address, date of birth, and a few other details, he or she could pose as you when signing up for an online service. Then if a background check is performed, it will confirm that the information he or she gave is correct—but it does not tell you that they are who they say they are.

To report a problem that arises with an eHarmony contact, send an e-mail to matchconcerns@eharmony.com. For general information about safety on eHarmony (and for sites that are similar to it), visit www.eharmony.com/safety/tips.

Verification Services

eHarmony works in partnership with RelyID.com and its affiliated company, backgroundchecks.com, to offer some ways for people to check up on certain details people report about themselves.

"It's pretty common for people on dating sites to not provide accurate information about themselves," says Pat Mangiacotti, vice president at backgroundchecks.com. "The younger the user, the more difficult it is to obtain certainty that the person is real," she said. "Once the person is over the age of 18, it gets easier."

The reason is that young adults begin to accumulate public records such as driver's licenses, credit and debit cards, and work histories. Services such as backgroundchecks.com maintain huge databases of public information and check what someone says against what is on the record.

This does not, though, guarantee that you are really dealing with a particular person. If someone had your name, date of birth, and a few of your numbers, he or she could fill out a form and pose as you in many situations—certainly on a dating site. Someone could get that information by stealing your wallet, for example.

Mangiacotti said her company goes beyond, serving up what she called "out of wallet" questions that can be verified from other public records and presumably would not be found out easily by someone who accidentally had a few bits of information about you. What was the color of your old car? Where have you lived in the past? What were the names of your roommates?

But Mangiacotti still advises caution. "Whether you're online or offline, you really need to have good judgment. You need to use common sense."

DON'T SHOW YOUR CARDS TOO SOON

As eHarmony points out, once you have revealed personal information—your address, your phone number, or some private details of your life—you cannot take it back. Go slowly and never allow yourself to be rushed.

One way to start direct communication without revealing more than you want is to set up an e-mail or instant messaging account just for "meeting" new people through online services. If someone misbehaves on that special account you can always stop using it and open another.

You can protect the privacy of your telephone number by making the call yourself instead of giving out your number; before you call, turn off the Caller ID on your home or cell phone. On most phone services, you can do that by punching in *67 before making a call; that will prevent the display of your number for the next call only. (The person you call will see something like "Private Call" or "Anonymous" instead of your name or phone number.

Be aware, though, that not all phone companies are able to completely block the display of your number. Test out your system by calling a friend who has Caller ID, or check with your phone company or cell phone service for advice.

DO YOUR OWN CHECKING

If someone gives you his or her name and a few other details, do some checking by yourself. Enter the name into a search engine such as Google.com and see what comes up.

You might find a posting somewhere from another person with a complaint. You might find a report about a criminal proceeding. You might find a newspaper story proclaiming the person as "Teen of the Year." Or you might find nothing at all.

Be careful with what you find. Remember that the Internet is like a gigantic pile of unsorted and mostly unverified information. Not everything you find there will be true, and sometimes there are horrible cases of mistaken identity. And it is also a surprise to most people to find that there may be dozens or hundreds of people who have the same name. The more details you have, the more specific a search you can conduct, but don't place 100 percent faith in what you find.

HOW TO MEET SOMEONE SAFELY

Pick a time and place to meet someone that will put both of you in a public place with lots of other people around. One great example is to meet for a lunch date. A bad example is midnight in a deserted park. You get the idea. Here are some other ways to keep things safe:

- ➤ Make the date short and agree on the schedule in advance. "Let's meet for lunch on Saturday at the Friendly's on Main Street. How about from noon to 1 P.M.?"
- ➤ Get to the date on your own. Have a friend or a trusted adult bring you, travel in your own car if you have one, or take a bus

or taxi. Don't get into your date's car the first time you meet him or her.

> Share the information about your plans with a trusted friend or member of the family. Tell where you are meeting and with whom, and promise to check in at an agreed-upon time after the date.

> Bring a fully charged cell phone with you.

> Keep your first dates simple and inexpensive. Be sure you discuss in advance who is paying any costs for meals or entertainment.

DO UNTO OTHERS

It is also important to understand that you should treat someone you meet online with respect, just the way they should treat you.

Don't badger people to do something they don't want to do, or to disclose information before they are ready. If you push someone, he or she might do the same to you.

And if someone you meet online decides not to meet you in person, don't make a big deal about it. Everyone you meet is not going to be perfect, and sometimes things don't work out.

Always be respectful and treat your matches as you would want them to treat you. Not every match is going to be right for you, so closing communication with matches and having matches close communication with you is a natural and healthy part of the process. eHarmony is about bringing two compatible people together who have a solid foundation from which a long-term relationship would have a high probability of success. You still need to consider carefully whether this particular person is one with whom you would like to further a relationship. If you feel the need to end communication, then be honest, direct, and polite. The sooner you address this determination, the better for both of you.

If a match feels the need to close communication with you, please respect the person's wishes.

Do not expect the online service to store your e-mails and IMs; most do not. For your own protection, though, you might want to keep your own copies of your conversations. Most IMs allow you to save a copy to a file, or you can cut and paste the conversation into a word processor.

On Match.com, the safety features include ways to use special e-mail addresses, instant messaging chats, and even telephone services that are routed through the company and do not require that you reveal your personal addresses or phone numbers.

Think twice or maybe three times before you try to attract attention to yourself by choosing a sexy or provocative user name. Is that

Signs Something May Be Wrong

Match.com includes in its safety tips a list of warning signs about some-one you meet on their service; they are adapted slightly for this book. Watch out for these, and more:

► If the other person will agree to speak with you only at strange times of the day or wants to meet in strange places, he or she may be keeping a secret. The person might be older or younger than claimed, or living in a situation that is different from what you understood (at home, or with their parents, or with someone else.)

► If you catch someone changing his or her story or just plain lying to you, think about this: If the person is are not honest with you at the start—before you've even met—what makes you think he or she will be honest if you become close?

► Beware of someone who gives vague or confusing answers to simple questions. It's a fine line here, but you need to learn the difference between someone who is being very cautious and someone who is trying to mislead you.

► Watch out for someone who declares love almost immediately. True love can happen any time but not usually within minutes after you meet. Your friend may be desperate, immature, unstable, or dishonest.

► Look out for someone who asks for money, complains about being cheated or swindled, or in any other way seems to want to involve you in something about money. Chances are it's your money he or she is after.

► Watch out for scammers. Be very careful not to click on Web links sent to you by someone you don't know. These could lead you to adults-only Web sites, or they might result in the download of a virus to your computer. Watch out, too, if someone asks you to call 1-900 phone numbers or phone numbers beginning with 976-xxxx. These are premium rate numbers that will automatically go on your phone bill (or your parents' bill) at very high cost.

Signing Off

If you do use your own e-mail account to send messages to someone you have met online, turn off any "signatures" that might include your mailing address or telephone number. If you need help in doing this, ask your Internet service provider for help or consult a trusted computer geek.

really the way you want someone to think of you before they've even met you? Do you think you might attract the wrong type of person, or perhaps scare away the right one?

WHAT YOU NEED TO KNOW

> Meeting someone online can be fun, and it does not require you to leave the safety of your home. But you have to be very careful about taking the next step from the Internet to the real world.

Calling for Support

An important way to protect yourself as well as all of the other users of a social Web site is to block any member who acts inappropriately and to notify the operator of the site. The company can try to keep them from bothering anyone else and can notify law-enforcement authorities if necessary.

Examples of people who should be blocked are adults who contact young people, young people who are trying to connect with adults, people who send harassing or offensive messages, and members who try to collect money or commit frauds. And, of course, you should notify the police and the company about any person who acts inappropriately in a face-to-face meeting.

Keep Your Head on Straight

People of any age, and especially teens, should never accept an alcoholic drink or drugs the first time they meet someone through a dating service. You need to stay sober and think clearly.

Also, sadly, when you are with someone you don't know, you should not accept a drink of any kind unless it comes in a sealed can or bottle. It is rare, but some criminals put drugs in drinks to take sexual advantage of people.

> ▸ Many friendship and dating sites require people to guarantee they are a particular age and to promise that the answers they give to other questions are true, but in most cases this information is not verified.
> ▸ Remember that not everyone is honest or has the best intentions. Some people lie about themselves. This happens on the Web and in the real world. Learn how to be careful.
> ▸ There are some things you can do for yourself to check on the background of people you meet, beginning with a basic Web search on their name.
> ▸ Watch out for people who push too hard, who ask for money, or ask you to get involved in their personal affairs. This is not proper behavior from someone you have just met and may be an indication that something is not proper.

9

Maintaining Your Identity

What is your identity? You could say it is your name, and that would be correct—up to a point. In our modern world of credit and debit cards, e-mail and text messages, social networks and online shopping, your identity is a wrapper around a whole package of information: your name, your banking information, your home address, your date of birth, your Social Security number, and your very existence in cyberspace.

There are no good reasons why someone would want to take over your identity. It's not an acceptable prank, and it's not funny.

The bad reasons? They include trying to steal money from your bank accounts, running up big bills on falsely obtained credit cards, or attempting to cause you embarrassment with your friends or family. It's also against the law.

If people had all or most of the information that makes up your identity, there is not much to keep them from acting as if they were you. They could obtain new or replacement credit cards, go shopping (and buy things you wouldn't purchase, even if you could afford to), apply for a job, mess up your online résumé, or establish a user name and pose as you on Facebook, Twitter, or any other Web site. But just consider this: What if someone chose to use your name to register an e-mail address and then sent nasty or humiliating e-mails or text messages to people you know? How about notes sent, signed as you, to your teachers or your boss?

IDENTITY THEFT: IT'S TOO EASY

Identity theft is relatively easy to accomplish for some things such as setting up an e-mail account. It's also not that difficult for someone to open a Facebook or other social networking site and claim to be you. And for a determined crook, it is not all that hard—if they have your information—to attempt to steal money from your accounts or to defraud a credit card company or a store.

According to the Federal Trade Commission, as many as 9 million Americans have their identities stolen each year. The bad news is that you may not even know about the problem until some bank, credit card company, or cell phone provider or (most annoying, a debt collector) starts asking you to pay for something you didn't buy.

The good news is that there are laws and regulations you can use to protect yourself against identity theft, and there are ways you can regain your good name if someone messes up your credit records.

The important news is that if you find that someone has stolen your identity and messed up your records, there are things you can (and must) do to set things right. You don't really have a choice; you have to take the time and make the effort. Otherwise, you could end up being turned down for college loans, find it impossible to get a

Shakespeare Had It Right

Shakespeare had no idea that one day we would live in a world of the Internet, cell phones, credit cards, and social networks. But he did know quite a bit about the value of a person's identity. In *Othello,* Iago says:

Good name in man and woman, dear my lord,
Is the immediate jewel of their souls.
Who steals my purse steals trash; 'tis something, nothing;
'Twas mine, 'tis his, and has been slave to thousands;
But he that filches from me my good name
Robs me of that which not enriches him,
And makes me poor indeed.

new credit card or take out a loan to buy a car, or even be turned away from a job because of bad marks on your record.

It all starts with being careful about how much of your personal identity you reveal and to whom.

HOW DOES SOMEONE GET YOUR PERSONAL INFORMATION?

There are three common ways someone can obtain personal information about you without your permission or knowledge. If you do not take care of your own information properly, some people at the very low end of the criminal world—"dumpster divers"—can look through your garbage in search of bills or other documents that have important details like your address and your account number. A notch up, or down if you prefer, is a thief. If someone steals your wallet—computer or cell phone—that person may be able to use the information and bank cards as if he or she were you.

Another way you might lose your personal information is if you are tricked into revealing it to someone who has no right to it. This includes online phishing sites that try to get people to reveal details. There are also ways for someone to snoop on your transactions made at a public Internet café. And if you allow your computer to pick up a virus, that program might be intended to search for details on your machine or record your typing at the keyboard and send it to a thief.

Finally, a company or individual that has your personal information might be sloppy in protecting the details it has on file. This includes break-ins to computer networks to steal customer files, something that happened repeatedly to several major retail and online stores in recent years. There is also a fraud called "pretexting," which means that someone has just enough information about you to claim to be you (under false pretenses, which is where the word *pretext* comes from) and then obtain things like your user name and password or the billing information from an account you have.

WHAT CAN IDENTITY THIEVES DO WITH YOUR INFORMATION?

Credit card fraud is one of the most common identity theft crimes. Thieves can use the information they know about you to open new credit card accounts in your name and then go on a spending spree. Or they can use your existing credit card information to make purchases, especially through online Web sites that require only the information on the card and not the piece of plastic itself.

Dealing with Dumpster Divers

As you get older and get a job, a bank account, and a driver's license, you will also begin to get mail–old-fashioned snail mail delivered in an envelope by the post office–that may contain bills or offers for credit cards or student loans.

Although you are not responsible if someone steals letters from your mailbox (that's a federal crime) or if someone obtains information about you from your trash, in either situation you could find your identity seriously messed up. Here are some things you can do to keep private information away from Dumpster divers:

▶ Clean out your mailbox regularly. If you are going away for a while, arrange for a trusted friend to collect your mail or contact the post office to have your mail held until you return.

▶ Open and destroy any junk mail that has personal information in it. Look for account numbers, birthdates, driver's license numbers, and that sort of data. Tear the section of the letter with information into little pieces.

▶ Be on the lookout for any bills or confirmation of accounts you did not open. If someone has been using your name, immediately contact the companies and inform them. Keep notes on your conversation and the names and confirmation numbers you receive. Ask a trusted adult to assist you.

In some schemes, the first thing a thief might do is notify the credit card company of a change of address; this might allow a month or even a few months to pass before you realize that someone is spending in your name.

If the information includes your bank account number, the thief might attempt to create counterfeit checks and spend your money. Your ATM or debit card should be safe . . . unless you made the terrible mistake of writing your PIN code on the back of the card or hiding it somewhere else in your wallet. You wouldn't do that, right?

A really nervy thief might try to use your information to obtain a driver's license or other official ID card that lists your name but has his or her picture. You may not know about this problem until you try

Protecting Your Wallet

The best way to guard against loss of the information in your wallet is to make sure you don't lose it or allow it to be stolen. The second-best way: Take a tour of your wallet every few weeks. Look for things that don't need to be with you all the time. For example, you don't need to carry your Social Security card; it may be necessary to present the card when you apply for or accept a job or when you visit the motor vehicle department to get a driver's license. The rest of the time it can be kept at home in a safe or in a file.

(By now, most states have stopped using Social Security numbers as the ID on driver's licenses; if you have the choice, ask the motor vehicle department to use its own numbers and not yours.)

Do not keep a plain language list of your passwords and user names in your wallet. What is plain language? That would be a list that anyone could easily understand, something like: "My Bank of East Overshoe account user name is TURTLEDOVE and my password is PANAMACANAL2397."

If you feel you absolutely must carry a list with you, put it in some kind of code. Let's say you included 2397 because it is the last four digits of your grandmother's telephone number. Your code list might say "PC+GG's L4."

You should also keep at home or somewhere out of your wallet a list of *the last four digits* of your credit or debit card numbers and the telephone numbers for customer service. You don't need the whole number to call them to report a theft.

to renew your real card. But if your wallet is lost or stolen, you should quickly notify your state's motor vehicle department and your school and anyone else who issues IDs.

PROTECTING YOURSELF FROM CREDIT CARD AND BANKING FRAUD

At the most basic level, be very careful before giving out your private information. Obviously, if you are applying for a credit card or opening a bank account, you are going to need to disclose data that allows the lender to check your history, and that usually includes your address, Social Security number and date of birth, and other details like bank accounts. But if someone sends you an e-mail offering a free chance at a sweepstakes lottery to win a pair of shoes, they don't need that kind of information; be very suspicious.

The second line of defense is to watch your bills carefully. When you get a credit card or banking statement, read it line by line. Even better: Check your accounts online at least once a week. Some banks and card companies allow you to set up automatic alerts that will send you an e-mail if especially large or unusual charges are spotted.

If you see something that looks wrong or something that is obviously fraud (you did not fly to Switzerland for a weekend of skiing and stop off at a jewelry store in Paris for some bling), you should immediately notify the bank or credit card company. Ask a trusted adult to assist you; it may be necessary to send a written letter challenging the charge.

If you receive a letter or an e-mail from a bank or credit card company (or anyone else) asking you to confirm that you have requested a change of address on your records . . . read it carefully. If you have not moved or requested that your statements be sent to a different address, something is wrong; someone may be trying to rip you off.

Do not respond to the e-mail; it may be an attempt at phishing. Do not send more information to an address in a letter; again, someone may be trying to trick you into doing something or revealing something that is not good for you. Instead, call the customer service telephone number for whatever company appears to have sent the letter or e-mail; find the phone number on a statement or from their Web page—not from any listing on what you have received.

If someone has attempted to change your billing address without your permission, you should ask all of the companies you deal with—banks and credit card companies especially—to close your existing accounts and issue you new numbers and cards. They may ask you to forward the mail you received so that they can examine it; if someone sent you an attempt at fraud in a letter delivered by the U.S. Postal Service, you may be asked to preserve the letter for a federal investigation.

The good news is that banks and credit card companies are required by federal law to work with you to immediately halt the damage from a lost or stolen card or the information that was on it. In nearly all cases, you will not be responsible for charges or withdrawals you did not make if you immediately notify the company as soon as you realize that there is a problem.

If your wallet is stolen or lost, call all of your banks and credit card companies immediately. Use the customer service number you will find on a statement you may have received or on a card you still have. Tell the person who answers the phone that you need to report the loss of a card or actual fraud; they will connect you to a special department to handle the situation.

If you don't know that someone has been using your information until you get a bill, call as soon as the bill arrives. The longer you wait, the more damage the thief can cause, and the greater the chances the bank or credit card company will give you grief over the charges. But in the end, you will be off the hook if you call quickly and cooperate in the investigation of anything that happens.

In most cases, you will have to follow up your phone call with a written and signed statement sent to any bank or lender where you are disputing fraud by others. The way it often works is that the company will take your report over the phone, shut down your existing accounts, and send you a statement you will need to sign and return by mail. (You might need to have your statement notarized; this is a process where someone recognized by the state as a notary witnesses you signing the document and examines identification cards you provide to prove you are who you say you are.)

If you are the victim of theft, you should also contact the police and file a report. That may help you in dealing with companies that think you owe them money. And just in case your wallet is ever found, they may be able to return it to you; even if they do, be sure to cancel all cards and get new accounts to protect yourself.

Be sure to be truthful in anything you say in a telephone call to your bank or lender, to a police officer, or in a signed statement. If what you tell them is false, you could end up in legal trouble. Consult with your parents or a trusted and knowledgeable adult if you have any questions about your situation and never agree to lie about the facts. (If you don't know the answer to a particular question, the best answer is: "I don't know.")

Once you have done all of your notifications, you should see whether your parents' or your own homeowners' or renters' or auto insurance policies include any protection against identity theft. They may be helpful in dealing with any claims and clearing up your credit record.

CLEANING UP A BAD CREDIT REPORT

You should understand that when you first get a credit card or obtain any kind of loan there will be someone (or at least a computer program) watching your spending and borrowing habits. Specifically, there are three major credit reporting agencies (Equifax, Experian, and Trans Union) that are used by almost all companies offering lines of credit; the information these companies hold is also consulted by some employers and landlords who may be considering giving you a job or renting you an apartment.

The credit report includes your life's history, basically focusing on two important measurements. The first, and most important when it comes to identity theft is this: Have you paid your bills on time?

The second important measurement on a credit report is a calculation of the percentage of your permissible total debt you are currently using. For example, if you have two credit cards, each with a credit line of $5,000, that means you are allowed to have as much as $10,000 owed; you can choose to pay off the full amount any time you receive a bill, or you might pay off only part of the amount owed and pay interest on the rest. The best customers are those with a large credit line and a small amount of debt.

Either way, if someone steals your identity and starts running up bills that you do not pay, it may end up affecting your credit report. Under federal law, you are entitled to check on your report once a year without charge; since there are three companies that collect very similar information, you might want to check in with a different agency every four months. To learn about how credit reports work, you can read a Web page at the Federal Trade Commission. Go to www.ftc.gov/bcp/edu/pubs/consumer/credit/cre34.shtm.

You can also go directly to a Web site that is maintained by the three major credit report companies and take a look at your credit report at any or all three of the companies. Be sure to follow the instructions carefully, and remember that you are entitled to a free report once a year from each of the companies. Do not sign up for any of the other services they will try to sell you: credit scores, automatic warning services, and additional reports among them. Unless you have run into serious problems because of identity theft, you can handle your own monitoring. To obtain a free report, go to www. annualcreditreport.com.

FILING AN IDENTITY THEFT REPORT

If someone steals your bicycle, your insurance company may want to see a police report of the theft before it offers to pay for your loss. If someone steals your name, the police are not going to be able to give it back to you, but filing a special Identity Theft Complaint Report may help to clean up your credit report and help protect you from the possibility of losing a job or a loan because of bad or incorrect information.

Begin by going to the Federal Trade Commission and locate its online Identity Theft Complaint Report. The easiest way to find it is to use an Internet search engine such as www.google.com or www.live.com and ask it to find Identity Theft Complaint Form.

Under federal law, the report gives you some valuable rights. Most important: The report can be used to permanently block fraudulent information appearing on your credit report that results from identity theft. For example, if someone takes your name and opens a credit account that is never paid off, that information will not be listed as your responsibility.

The Identity Theft Complaint Report is also needed to place an extended fraud alert on your credit report. This is a notice to lenders that someone—not you—attempted fraud using your name; it should reduce the chances of future problems.

There are three steps here: File an Identity Theft Complaint Report online with the FTC; print out a copy; then bring the printout to the police to be included as part of a police report.

Some police departments may be very helpful when you ask to file an Identity Theft Complaint Report; others may try to tell you that they are too busy with more important crimes. Ask your parents or a trusted adult to help you in politely insisting they take your report. You can also contact the office of the attorney general in your state (you can find a telephone number by searching on the Internet or by going directly to www.naag.org) to see if there are state laws requir-

Better Safe Than Sorry

If you have notified all of your credit card and bank companies of the loss or theft of your information and they have removed all disputed charges from your existing accounts, you may not need to file an Identity Theft Complaint Report. If no one is asking you to pay charges that are fraudulent, there is no information to be recorded on your credit record. But do not hesitate to file a report if someone has opened new accounts in your name or if debt collection services are trying to get you to pay for charges that are not yours.

ing your police department to take the report, or if there is a state agency or state police office that could assist you. Check the Blue Pages of your telephone directory for the phone number, or check for a list of state attorneys general.

If the police are reluctant to take your report, ask to file a Miscellaneous Incident report, or try another jurisdiction, like your state police. Ask for a copy of the police report. If you are told you cannot have the report, be sure to obtain the report number as well as the name of the officer who prepared it.

PLACING A FRAUD ALERT

Putting a fraud alert on your credit report can prevent someone from opening new accounts in your name; lenders will see a notice that you have been the victim of identity theft and will either refuse to open new accounts or attempt to contact you to verify personal details. The alert might even allow lenders to work with police to make an arrest.

To add an alert to your report, make a phone call to any one of the three credit report companies; by federal law they are required to contact the other two companies on your behalf. It does not hurt to call all three, and you should do that if you do not receive a written confirmation from each of them.

Equifax: (800) 525-6285. www.equifax.com
Experian: (888) 397-3742. www.experian.com
TransUnion: (800) 680-7289. www.transunion.com

After the alert has been filed, you are entitled to a free copy of your credit report from each of the companies, even if you had looked at your report within the past year. Examine the report carefully for any accounts you did not open, any debts you believe you do not owe, and any inquiries about you from companies you have not contacted.

If you find something that looks wrong, call each of the reporting companies and ask to speak with the security or fraud department; discuss each problem you have found. You will then have to send a signed letter repeating the details of what you have found, or you will receive a statement from the credit report company based on your phone call and be asked to sign and return it to them.

Make notes on the date and time and the name of each person you speak to, and keep copies of all letters or forms you send regarding your situation.

GOING FORWARD

When the dust settles, you will probably receive new credit cards or debit cards, and your bank account numbers may change. Be sure to assign new user names, passwords, and PINs to all of your accounts; do not recycle old ones.

If you have successfully dealt with a lender or a bank to remove fraudulent claims, ask that they send a letter stating that they have removed the fake charges and closed the accounts. Keep that letter in a safe place in case you ever need to deal with the credit bureau or another lender about the situation.

The basic fraud alert will stay on your credit report for at least 90 days. That is probably more than enough time to allow you to obtain new accounts and block any attempt by thieves to use your name; in most cases, they'll move on to new victims very quickly.

But in more serious cases, where there has been actual fraud committed, you should ask the credit bureaus to place an "extended fraud alert" on your record. This will be in place for seven years or until you request it be removed; if you file an Identity Theft Complaint Report with the FTC, the extended alert should be automatically put in place. While this is on your record, new lenders are required to contact you or meet with you in person before any new credit accounts are created.

Finally, a number of states also have laws that allow you to freeze access to your credit report. This does not mean that the agency will not continue to collect information about you and your dealings with lenders and banks. Instead, it means that no one can see or use your report without your permission. You would have to unfreeze your report if you apply for a loan or credit card, or if you want to allow an employer to check your record. Contact your state's attorney general to find out if there is such a law to freeze reports in your location.

ABOUT PASSWORDS AND REMINDERS

The first rule of passwords is to make them hard for someone to guess. That celebrity—with the first name of the capital city of France and the last name of the hotel chain that was the source of her money—found her cell phone account easily hacked because her pet Chihuahua was almost as famous as she was.

If one of your friends (or someone you thought was your friend) tried to break into your online accounts, don't you think he or she would try guessing your password with the name of your dog or cat or your favorite baseball team? Other obvious passwords might include your telephone number, middle name, nickname, or favorite color.

The problem is that for many of us a great deal of personal information is spread around on the Internet. If you have a Facebook or MySpace page, does your profile or blog discuss your favorite actor or the color of your new shoes? Is your telephone number listed in the phone book? Is it available through an Internet search?

Even your Social Security number or your driver's license number is not secret. How many times have you revealed that information, and what makes you think it was never seen by people you don't trust? If a thief wanted to hack into your account, these tidbits would be the obvious places to start.

HOW TO CONSTRUCT A TOUGH PASSWORD

Rule one: Make the password something unique to you. Put together the names of two very different people—friends, movie stars, famous athletes—and separate them by a number that is not directly associated with you (no birthdays, please.) Just as an example, I might choose the number 1609 because that was the year Henry Hudson sailed up the river in New York and I once wrote a book about the explorer. I pick the names Kevin and Dustin from the Red Sox and come up with this password: Kevin1609Dustin.

That particular password is pretty strong, and I could even make a note to myself to help remember without worrying about someone figuring it out. My note might say, 1BHH2B to remind me that I used the first baseman, Hudson, and the second baseman to construct a password.

Another scheme you might use for your passwords is to use the telephone number for someone or something completely unrelated to you. For example, you might use the number for a local pizzeria; if you ever forget the number, you can look it up in the phone book. Or you could use the number for a distant relative (not your own number or your parents', which someone could guess). Got an aunt in Albuquerque or an uncle in Utica?

Rule two: Use a different password for each account you establish.

Rule three: Change your password at least every few months, and immediately any time you suspect or know that someone has gotten hold of it.

Rule four, related to rule three: Never tell anyone your password, with one exception. Some parents will ask their children to give them their user name and passwords for social Web sites like Facebook with the promise that this information will never, ever be used unless there is a real emergency that involves your safety.

HOW TO AVOID THE PASSWORD RESET TRAP

What happens if you forget your password to a banking Web site, to a social networking site, or to a shopping site? The good news is that most Web sites will be happy to assist you in "recovering" your password or your user name. The bad news is that some of the ways they help you are not very secure at all.

When you register an account with many sites, they will ask you to fill out several "hint" questions that can be used later on to prove you are who you say you are. For example, the site might ask questions like these:

1. What is your mother's maiden name?
2. What is your father's year of birth?
3. What high school did you attend?

Those might sound like tough questions for someone to guess, but a determined criminal could find out the answer to all three of them with just a bit of poking around in public records or on the Internet.

But if you're clever, why not give your brain a little exercise in creative writing. It's a bit like writing a short story or creating an alter ego. Invent a new family that is just for the purposes of passwords and user names: a mother and father and grandparents, cars, schools, pets, honeymoons and vacations, and favorite colors, sports teams, and foods. Come up with a really strange family, even weirder than your own: Montezuma and Pigpen Hiccup, who live in East Overshoe, drive a Hupmobile, and enjoy eating deep-fried catcher's mitts.

Do not use *any* of the information in your short story for user names or passwords. Your imaginary family is only for filling out the hint sections of Web sites. By creating this made-up family, you are protecting yourself against the chance of anyone guessing your password reset hints. But just as you should do with your actual user names and passwords, you should change your hints every few months or any time you find out (or believe) that your privacy has been invaded.

USING A MASTER PASSWORD VAULT

Another way to protect your passwords and user names is to use a password vault. These are utility programs that are built into some Internet browsers or sold as part of antivirus or security programs.

One example is Identity Safe, included as part of Symantec's Norton 360 product.

The key to using this sort of product is to come up with one really secure master password that you can remember. Make it as long and complex as possible. Then change all of your actual passwords for Web sites to complete gibberish and don't even try to remember them. For example, your banking password could be 29048uerjiopk and your MySpace password JIJKuiji7887x.

Let the password vault worry about remembering the unmemorable and nearly impossible-to-guess secret codes. But you should still plan on changing them every six months or so.

WHAT YOU NEED TO KNOW

➤ If you find that someone has gotten hold of your personal information, including credit or debit cards, your Social Security number, your driver's license, your date of birth, don't wait: Contact your bank or credit card company and let them know. They may freeze your accounts or change the numbers.

➤ Keep copies of the customer service phone numbers and the last four digits of your accounts. That's all you need to call in a report in case of a loss or theft.

➤ Examine letters before you throw them out. Make sure they do not contain information that would allow a stranger to pose as you. Be sure you completely destroy any full account numbers or other personal information.

➤ Read your incoming bills carefully and immediately contact the company if you see a charge you do not recognize.

➤ Once you are old enough to have your own credit cards or loans, check your credit report every few months to make sure it is accurate.

➤ The secret to a good password is to come up with something so obscure that it could not be guessed by someone who knows you well or by someone who has researched the publicly available information about you.

➤ One good source for passwords is to use a telephone number of someone or something completely unrelated to you. If you forget the password, you can look it up, but it would be nearly impossible for someone to guess it.

➤ Choose difficult questions for password reminders used by some Web site. Otherwise, you are allowing someone the chance to get into your account by resetting a forgotten password.

10

Viruses: A Computer Can Develop a Cold

Got a computer? Use the Internet? Then someone is trying to ruin your day.

It's about as simple as that. Any computer hooked up to the Net in any way is regularly being exposed to nasty viruses, spyware, adware, and other unpleasant insults.

It's a sad thing that some people feel they have to cause other people problems or otherwise interfere with their lives. These are the same types of people who feel they need to express themselves by spray-painting graffiti on a freshly painted wall or knock down mailboxes with a baseball bat. It's obnoxious, it's malicious, and it's a fact of life.

A quick explanation is in order here. A computer virus is a piece of software that makes your computer do something you don't want it to. It's not alive like a germ, but it does act in many ways like diseases that pass from one human to another.

Think about the world we humans live in. Bacteria, viruses, and other sources of infection are all around us. We all learn—some better than others—how to keep ourselves healthy. If we can, we avoid going to places that are infected or meeting people who are contagious. We protect ourselves with things like vitamins and vaccinations. And when we somehow still come down with the flu, we visit the doctor and seek special treatment to remove the invader from our bodies.

Keep that in mind as we explore how computer viruses can make their way into your computer and the things we can do to remove them and keep them away.

HOW COMPUTERS BECOME INFECTED

When you buy a brand-new computer, plug it in, and turn it on, in theory you have a clean and uninfected machine. Modern computer makers are pretty good about inspecting every piece of software they install at the factory. The real threat comes when the new machine is exposed to other "mean" computers. That can happen in any of the following ways:

When you install a new piece of software on your computer. Two common sources of danger are "freeware" or "shareware," which are programs given away or sold on the honor system by individuals or companies. And especially dangerous: "warez," the unauthorized or illegal sale or giveaway of commercial software in violation of the developer's copyright.

When you add to your system bootleg or file-sharing copies of music or video. Although it may seem like a cool thing to share the latest tracks from a CD, an MP3 from a music Web site, or a video version of a hit movie or television show, it is also possible to pick up a virus along with your entertainment.

When you connect your computer to another computer over a local network. In many homes, schools, and places of business, computers can work together over a network to exchange files or share hardware like a printer or a large hard-disk drive. (One common type of network is often referred to as an Ethernet.) Any time your computer is on a network, it is at risk of picking up any infection that has taken hold on any other attached machine.

When you connect to the Internet. The Internet, also called the Web, is basically a huge international network of computers. There is no license required to drive on the information superhighway; all you need is a computer (or a cell phone or a Blackberry or something like those devices) and a connection to the Internet. Those connections can be over a regular telephone (dial-up service), over a specialized phone line (DSL), or through a dedicated cable (provided by a cable television company or sometimes by a phone company.) Once you are on the Internet, your little machine is swimming in a sea of information, music, video . . . and sewage.

When you attach to the Internet by WiFi. A wireless connection between your laptop or cell phone and another computer or a wireless modem is a substitute for a cable. This presents two separate threats. First, there is the possibility that another machine or another user may find a way to listen in on your radio communication or insert something nasty into the stream. Second, once the connection is made to the Internet, your machine is up against the same sort of threats faced by a computer that connects directly by wire.

When you visit a Web site that harbors infectious material. In the wild world of the Internet, this can be just about any site. However, the sites that are least likely to be infected are those that are run by major commercial or governmental organizations; they guard their sites from intrusion and inspect them constantly. The sites most likely to be infectious are either those that are set up specifically to spread viruses or steal information or those that are basically unmanaged. That's why file-sharing sites offering pirated or unauthorized copies of programs, music, or videos are especially dangerous.

If you are phished or conned. If someone sends you an e-mail that includes a link to a Web site, how do you know that you are not being sent to a place that will infect your system with a virus?

PROTECTING YOUR MACHINE AND YOUR STUFF

Although some fans of Apple Computer's Macintosh operating system claim their machines are completely safe from intrusion by a virus, that is not quite true. There are many more threats to PCs than Macs, but there are also many more PCs in use. In recent times, some virus writers have begun to turn their attention toward Macs. Whatever the maker of your computer or the operating system it runs, there are several very important steps you should take to protect your system and the data you keep within it.

Always use a current version of the operating system for your machine. That doesn't mean you have to use the latest version, just one that is still supported and still updated on a regular basis by the manufacturer. If you don't know which versions are still being kept up to date, contact the maker of your operating system (Microsoft and Apple are the two largest companies) or consult a knowledgeable computer expert. You're not asking for an opinion here, just the facts.

Do not use a pirated, unauthorized, unlicensed, or otherwise unofficial version of an operating system. Everyone likes

What's a patch? In theory, an update is software that improves the ability of the operating system to do what it is supposed to do. A patch is software intended to repair a problem. Sometimes, though, these are differences without a distinction. There are also upgrades; these are supposed to be changes to your operating system or other software that add completely new features. If there is a newly discovered security threat, the operating system has to be adjusted, and it doesn't matter whether the solution is called an update or a patch, or whether there is a new upgrade released that just happens to repair a security problem. In the end, all that matters is that the fix is in.

to save a few dollars, but buying software in a plain brown envelope from a guy with a table out back of the barbecue restaurant is not a smart way to equip your machine. A bootleg copy of an operating system may or may not contain a virus (or alterations that allow a virus to take hold), but you may very well find that the real maker of the product will refuse to update or support a version that does not have a valid serial number or other form of verification.

Keep your operating system updated. Microsoft Windows and Apple's OS both allow your machine to contact the maker and obtain and install updates and patches. This is very easy to do if your machine is constantly or regularly connected to the Internet; just instruct the operating system to check for updates.

Use a firewall. This is a piece of software or hardware that sits between your computer and the outside world. Think of this as an electronic security guard that sits outside your house checking IDs and turning away the obvious riffraff. The value of a firewall is that it does a pretty good job of recognizing—and turning away—attempts by evildoers to rattle the doorknob on every PC they can find on the Internet. A firewall aims to keep all of the doors locked, except for those visitors you tell it to allow. Many pieces of networking hardware, like routers or gateways, include a firewall. Most operating systems, including current versions of Microsoft Windows, have a software equivalent. In most cases, you can have both a hardware and software firewall in place.

Purchase, install, and keep current an antivirus program. These utilities exist on the inside of any firewall you have; they are there to deal with threats that make it past the security guards. There are a number of antivirus programs that do a pretty good job of inspecting your system as it exists when you install them and then standing on guard against future attempts at intrusion. They do their work inside your computer, usually as an extension of your operating system, keeping an eye on any programs that are on its list of threats or that seem to be like those a virus might attempt. The most popular products include the Norton products from Symantec Corporation (www.symantec.com) and those from McAfee, Inc. (www.mcafee.com). You'll also find highly rated products from Kaspersky Lab (http://usa.kaspersky.com) and Bitdefender (www.bitdefender.com). Before you spend money on one of these products, check to see if your Internet provider or the maker of your PC offers a free or discounted version.

Set up the antivirus program properly. Nearly all of the programs come with automatic installation and configuration "wizards" that turn on all of the appropriate safeguards. Some antivirus programs are part of a larger package of security utilities, and they may offer their own software firewall; in that case, you may be asked to choose between the one that comes with your operating system or the one that is in the utility. Start by following the recommendations of the security software company; if you find that your computer does not seem to be working properly, you can always loosen some of the strings and go back to the way the operating system maker recommends you set up your machine.

Make sure your antivirus utility works together with your e-mail program to examine mail that comes in and goes out of your machine. Here's a warning, though: The antivirus should be able to spot a virus or spyware that is part of any message you receive, but it won't be able to determine if any "click here" links in a message take you to a dangerous page. If you do find yourself on a Web site that is trying to download something nasty to your machine, you should be able to rely on the antivirus program to detect its arrival.

Follow the rules proposed by the maker of your antivirus program. Most programs allow you to instruct them on just how tightly you want them to clamp down on files that come in to your machine or on certain activities your machine might be asked to perform. For example, the antivirus could watch for any command that says "erase a program" or "change the operating system's settings" and immediately put on the brakes to ask you if that is something you really want to allow to happen. Depending on how sophisticated you are when it comes to computers and the Web sites you visit as well as e-mail you receive, you can look for the best combination of security and freedom for you and your PC.

Look left, look right, and scan. Make sure your antivirus program is instructed to conduct regular scans of the entire system at least once a month; if you visit dangerous sites, you might want to scan more frequently. Depending on how large the hard disk in your machine is, a scan can take a few hours; you might want to start the scan at the end of the day and leave it to work through the night. Some current antivirus programs work by themselves in the background, checking portions of your system any time they can find a few minutes of free time; they'll scan during your lunch, while you're on the phone, and even when you're just sitting there staring at the screen and not asking the computer to do something.

Perform an individual scan on any file that arrives by e-mail or is given to you in any form other than in a sealed cardboard box from a factory. Always assume that such casually transferred files may have been exposed to viruses. Nearly all antivirus programs allow you to identify a specific file in an e-mail or in a directory on your hard disk and inspect it for signs of problems.

DETERMINING IF YOUR COMPUTER HAS A VIRUS

The doctor is in. Here are a few questions to help you diagnose whether your computer is sick:

Is it working noticeably slower than it used to? There are a number of reasons why this could be happening; none of them has anything to do with using lower-quality electricity or whether the moon is full or new.

Is your computer's hard disk full, or nearly full? If you have been adding lots of pictures, videos, or music recently, you may be using so much space that the machine no longer has enough space to "think."

More Room for Your Stuff

If you need assistance in figuring out how much space remains on your hard-disk drive, whether it is fragmented, or how to add more storage, I'd suggest you buy a how-to book about your machine or its operating system (I've written more than a few), or consult with a knowledgeable computer user. It's not that complicated, but it's not really the subject of this book, either.

Although most PCs and Macs use their RAM (memory) to hold files that you are working on right now, many machines also allow software programs to use part of available disk space (storage) as a temporary place for work in progress, kind of a spillover. Under Microsoft Windows, this is sometimes called "virtual memory."

In general, I recommend that you never allow your hard drive to become more than three-quarters full. If its capacity is 200GB, that means it should not be filled above 150GB. If your machine runs out of virtual memory, it will slow down anytime you try to work with a big file.

Another thing that can happen is that your hard drive can become "fragmented," meaning that pieces of the same file are scattered all over the disk instead of in one, easy-to-find-and-use place. Severe fragmentation can also slow down your machine.

Remember that in most systems when you "delete" a file, it isn't necessarily erased from your computer's hard drive. Instead, it may be placed in a "recycle bin," where it still takes up space until you instruct the system to actually erase it from storage or until a new file is stored where the old data had formerly resided.

What have you changed since the last time the computer worked properly? That is the basic question you should ask anytime your PC or your cell phone or your music player or any other piece of electronics suddenly seems more like a brick than a stealth fighter.

If you have made a change to a setting, try to go back to how it was before. If you have installed a new program, think about uninstalling it. If you have upgraded a program, it may have glommed onto a lot more space than the previous edition.

Is your computer's hard drive acting strangely, churning away at times when it used to be silent? You may be able to see an indication of activity if your computer has a light that flashes or pulses when the drive is in use, or you may notice the sounds of the spinning drive.

There may be an innocent explanation. Some computers are set up to perform automatic antivirus scans, or defragmentation on a specified schedule. Also, if your computer is attached to a local network and someone else is accessing files that are on your machine's hard-disk drive, you're going to see activity for as long as the drive is needed.

But if that is not your situation, then there may be a more sinister situation. A hacker may have managed to get through whatever firewalls or antivirus protection you have on your machine (or waltzed right through the open door to an unguarded machine) and installed a "zombie" or "spyware" or other types of unwanted invaders.

A zombie is a piece of software that uses your computer to launch attacks on others, or to uses the contents of your address book to send barrages of e-mails selling garbage (and worse) or attempting to spread itself to other machines, using yours as its base. Spyware is a more direct attempt at thievery, launching a search of your computer for information such as bank account or credit card numbers.

Are things getting just plain weird? No, I'm not talking about the guy at school who has taken to wearing a wizard's hat or your kid sister who has decided to follow you around and do everything you do, only not nearly so well.

Here are some weird things that might indicate a virus has landed on your computer's hard drive: Files are seeming to disappear all by themselves; file names are changing, sometimes with the insertion of nonsense or naughty words; or strange and unexpected messages are appearing on your screen.

Is your antivirus program or other security program displaying a warning message? If your antivirus or security program is telling you that it has either found a virus or detected viruslike activity? That's a pretty good clue that something has gone wrong.

GETTING RID OF A VIRUS

If you have installed an antivirus or security program, properly set it up, and kept it up to date, the process of removing most viruses is relatively easy. Most of these programs will do the job automatically.

Depending on the product you use and the instructions you gave it at setup, it should either detect and remove the virus from your machine or detect and quarantine the bug. Both options should prevent further damage to your machine. Putting a virus into quarantine is sort of like locking it up in a safe; it's still there, but it can't get out unless you release it.

Why would you want to quarantine a virus rather than just delete it? First, there is always the possibility that your antivirus software has mistaken a legitimate, nondestructive program for a virus. That used to be more of a problem years ago, but if it happens, all you need to do is release the program from captivity. (If you have any doubts, call or contact the antivirus maker for assistance before taking any chances.)

The second reason some antivirus programs use a quarantine is that a legitimate file—perhaps part of the software that powers your word processor or music player—has been infected. In some situations, it may be possible for the antivirus program to perform surgery on the file and remove the bad code. Again, follow any instructions very carefully to avoid making a bad problem worse.

The other way to remove viruses is to keep in regular contact with the maker of your operating system. Microsoft, for example, regularly releases "malware" removal tools for nasty programs that get past protections; at the same time, they usually also patch Windows to close the door to the latest threats.

WHAT YOU NEED TO KNOW

> If your computer is connected to the Internet, to another machine, or if you load software or files received from anyone else, it is at risk of being infected by a virus. Malware can come in through just about any door opened to the outside world.

> There are many more PCs in use than Macs, and it is mostly for that reason that there are many more PC viruses. All computers should be protected by current operating systems and utilities, and you should follow the rules for safe computing no matter what brand of computer you use.

> Keep your operating system and antivirus software up to date, and use them to scan your computer regularly.

> If your machine begins to run very slowly or show strange behavior, consider the possibility that it has been infected. Scan your system.

11

Don't Click on That Link

Have you seen the latest prankster video on YouTube? Want to see photos from backstage at the hottest concert of the year? Congratulations: $1 million dollars is waiting for you.

Wait! Don't click on that link.

Unless you know the person sending you an e-mail or have requested information from a legitimate Web site, you should always be very careful about clicking on a link in a message you have received.

The same goes for any "pop-up" message that appears on your screen when you visit a Web site. ("You are the millionth customer this year. Click here to claim your prize!) How come you are always the millionth?

These may be perfectly harmless bits of exaggerated advertising—or they may be nasty traps waiting to open up a can of computer-whupping.

Links in an e-mail address can be as simple as the name of a legitimate Web site, let's say www.youtube.com, just as an example. But they could also connect your computer to a site programmed to download a virus or other unpleasantries.

Remember this as you use the Internet: In most situations, any time you visit a Web site the owner of that location in cyberspace is able to determine the Internet address of your computer and sometimes more information about your machine and about you. If you have a software or hardware firewall and an antivirus program in place, you've got the basic level of protection. But depending on how your security program is set up, you may be instructing the electronic guardians to stand aside and let in the new stuff.

In general, be careful with any e-mail you receive that has "active" content—something that wants to do something on your computer. These include such things as animated birthday or holiday cards, screensavers, or cute little smiley-face cursors.

If the message says that the card was sent to you by a person you know and trust, and if it makes sense for you to receive it (your birthday is coming up or just passed), you might be safe in accepting the card. But if you don't know the sender, if the card is addressed to "undisclosed recipients" or to a name you don't recognize, or if there is anything at all odd about the message such as unusual phrases that sound like they were written by a foreigner or an amateur, delete the mail without touching the link or responding in any way.

One of the more devious scams reported in the computer press swept through offices a few years ago. People received e-mails that promised them freebies or jokes or pictures . . . anything to get them to click on the link. When they did, they were directed to what appeared to be a real Web site. What they didn't expect to receive was an e-mail (with information collected when they visited the Web site) that threatened to alert their boss that they had used the company computer to go to a pornography page. It was an attempt at extortion—forcing someone to pay money to keep something secret—for an event that didn't really happen.

No Privacy in Public

If you use a computer in school, at the library, or at your job, you should always remember that the owner of a computer or a computer network has the ability (and the right) to keep track of all Web sites that are visited and all e-mails sent and received through company accounts. If you get a job after school working at a shoe store, don't visit X-rated sites, gambling pages, or even innocent social networking sites without understanding that your boss just might find out. You could lose your job in a hurry if you violate company rules.

Hidden E-mail Dangers

There is another type of message you may receive in your in-box. It would appear blank on your screen or with just a few words like "Important" or "Special Offer." At the top of the message, your e-mail program might have a notice like this: "Some pictures have been blocked to prevent the sender from identifying your computer. Click here to download pictures."

And the message itself may have another notice: "Having trouble viewing this e-mail? Click here."

Please don't click. What you've received is an e-mail that consists of a picture or other type of image instead of words.

This sort of message *may* be legitimate and safe, or it may be an attempt by someone to get you to download something other than a picture: a virus, perhaps. Look at the information on your screen. Who is the sender? Do you recognize the name of the person or the company? Who is the message sent to? Do you see your name, or does it list "undisclosed recipients" or something else like that?

For "click here" to display a message e-mail, follow this theory: When in doubt, throw it out. If you're not in doubt, proceed cautiously.

At the end of 2008, another version of e-mail scamming swept through the Internet. Messages were sent out appearing to come from one or another of the major airline companies, including American Airlines, Continental, Delta, and JetBlue. Various versions of the ripoff used messages that said there was money due for an airline ticket, that there was a refund for overpayment, or that there was confirmation of an upcoming airline flight. Even people who had no plans to take a flight looked at the message and thought it might be important.

Now comes the problem: Instead of merely disclosing information, the message asked people to click on a link to download a file of information. The file was a Zip (a type of file that is electronically squeezed to make it as small as possible). There are all sorts of good reasons to send Zips instead of larger files—they upload and download faster, and they take up less room on a hard drive. But the problem is that when you "unzip" one of these files you are allowing a program to run on your computer, and some virus writers have used this as a way to sneak junk onto clean machines.

Once again, the same advice applies. If the message is obviously wrong (wrong name, misspellings, improper words), throw it away. If it looks like it might be for real, make sure that your antivirus software is running and up to date before you click on the message. The security software should be able to stop most attacks once they begin.

HOW TO SPOT A SUSPICIOUS PACKAGE

Many sites you visit inform you that you need to download and install an "ActiveX" or other type of mini program in order to continue. In theory, this is okay; these are special features (sometimes called "applets") that allow your computer to do something new. It may add a game or a music or video player. Or the applet may be intended to scan your computer to find problems.

However, as we have seen throughout this book, there are always some people who choose to mess things up for the rest of us.

There is really no way in advance to know what an ActiveX or other such download will really do on your machine until it is let loose. Start by looking carefully at the information on the screen that asks you for permission to download something. Here are the questions to ask yourself:

1. Did you choose to go to a Web site and download a program, or did this offer just seem to pop up out of nowhere? If you went to a site—perhaps to download a new Web browser or a music or video player—at least you know the reason for the screen.
2. Is the message warning you about something for which you are already protected? If you have an antivirus program on your computer and then you receive a pop-up or an e-mail saying something like, "Warning: Your computer may be infected," examine the message carefully. Is it from your antivirus program, or is it coming in over the Internet? If it is from outside your machine, it is probably someone trying to sell you something . . . and possibly someone trying to infect your computer. Do not accept it.
3. Do you recognize the name of the company that publishes the program? If the publisher name is blank, do not download the applet. If there is a name but you do not recognize it, think twice before accepting the download.

Make No Exceptions

There's an old joke about retailing that also makes a good point about the dangers of clicking on a link from someone you don't know or trust.

There's this guy standing on the street in back of a table with one perfectly red, polished apple on a platter. The sign says: "Apple: One million dollars."

Someone comes up to the guy and asks: "How in the world do you expect to make a living selling an apple for that ridiculous price?" And the guy answers: "I only need one customer."

That's the problem with some of the nasty Web sites and links you may see on your screen. If you say "no" to all of them, you and your machine should be pretty safe. But if you say "yes" to just one bad apple, not only could it bring in a bad virus or malware, but it could also prop open the Internet door on your computer to allow an entire menagerie of strange and misbehaving creatures.

Once again, this important advice: Make sure you have a current antivirus or security program on your computer. If you do end up allowing a nasty applet to come through, these steps should stop it in its tracks before much or any damage is done.

FREE PROGRAMS AND SHAREWARE

Why would a person or a company go to the trouble of writing and then distributing a piece of software and then offer it for free?

Some people truly do enjoy seeing their work spread around the world and don't expect payment of any kind from any one. In the early days of personal computers, that was fairly common; it was a way for people to brag about how clever they were.

Then there are some companies that offer free software and hope to make money through the sale of ads that are displayed to users. That's the case with products like Google, for example. You might find it acceptable to see a few ads on a Web page you visit. But you might not be happy if the program causes your screen to fill with pop-up ads.

Other companies will give away a game or a ringtone or a little utility in exchange for information: your telephone number, your e-mail address, or even more. Think before you make this trade: Do you really want to get even more spam in your e-mail account or phone calls from people selling things? Of course, some people set up special e-mail accounts that they use only for offers like this, keeping junk away from important messages.

Some companies give away software to users to help them sell software to other programmers. That's the case with some Microsoft products, including Internet Explorer.

Then there are the crooks. Some try to trick you into downloading free products so that they can get onto your computer or digital device and then try to steal your personal information.

Finally, there are some people who believe they have the right, or at least the ability, to give away copies of anything they can put their hands on. They will tell you that software should be free or that music belongs to everyone. That's a nice idea, but the fact is that authors of programs, music, and books need to pay their bills. There are laws that allow copyright owners to go after people who take material without permission. And, depending on your point of view, there's

A Credit Card Company Gets Phished

In 2009, *Wired* magazine reported about a security problem that hit some 500 employees of the credit card company Capital One. According to the story, the employees received an e-mail that seemed to be a legitimate request from a reporter asking for an interview. It included a link that was supposed to refer to another article about the company.

About 125 of the people who received the e-mail clicked on the link, and when they did, all they saw on their computer screen was a blank Web page. But while they stared at it and tried to figure out what was going on, the Web site was sending a virus back down the wire; since the employees had "asked" for the information by clicking on the link, the malware got right through the firewall on the company's system.

an even worse possibility: Unmanaged file-sharing sites are often the source of viruses and malware mixed in with the freebies.

WHAT YOU NEED TO KNOW

➤ Always be cautious before accepting a download of any file or program over the Internet. If the file is a complete surprise to you, assume that it is dangerous or fraudulent until you can prove otherwise. In any case, never accept a download without having a current version of an antivirus program running on your computer.

➤ In nearly every case, when you visit a site on the Internet, the operators of that location are able to determine your computer's address on the Web and perhaps other bits of information about you or your machine. Again, a good security program will minimize the chances that private details will leak out in this way.

➤ When you use a public computer at school or a library, or a machine owned by your employer, you have no guarantee of privacy when it comes to the sites you visit or the mail you send.

12

Cell Phones, IMs, and Text Messaging

Once upon a time, when people went to school or for a drive in the car or on vacation, they were out of touch. If they absolutely had to call someone, they would look for a phone booth and fish a nickel or a dime out of their pocket and dial the number.

Today, instead of taking a coin out of our pockets, we grab a cell phone half the size of a deck of cards. It works almost all the time and just about everywhere.

For better or for worse, almost everyone can be reached by phone any time from any place. The better part? We're never out of touch. When traveling, we can take our telephones with us and manage our personal and work matters. The worse part? We're never out of touch. There used to be whole parts of the day or even days at a time when you could get away from your worries. Now if people try to reach you by cell phone and you don't answer, they start thinking about calling the search-and-rescue squad.

Although most of us still call them cell phones, which refers to their original single purpose as a mobile replacement for a wired telephone, modern devices offer much, much more. Today, an ordinary cell phone also allows you to send and receive text messages, take and transmit digital pictures, play games, and listen to music. The most advanced "phones," devices including Apple's iPhone and RIM's Blackberry (and their growing group of competitors), have added things such as access to Web sites on the Internet, streaming video and audio coming over the Net, GPS direction-finding for driv-

Can You Hear Me Now?

At the start of 2009, the estimated population of the entire planet was about 6.7 billion people. And as the year began, the total number of cell phone subscribers was about 3.3 billion, or nearly exactly 50 percent of the global population.

In the developed world, if you take out of consideration the very young and the very old, it becomes harder and harder to find someone who doesn't have a cell phone. In the United States, the number of subscribers is equal to more than 82 percent of the population. Of course, as with any statistic, you have to read the fine print carefully; perhaps 20 percent of Americans have more than one cell phone. You can't go very far without finding someone blabbering away or clicking madly to send a text message.

By most estimates, cell phones were the most quickly adopted technology in the history of humankind. From the time they were first available—in Europe and the United States sometime around 1994—they were an immediate hit. They moved into homes and pockets at a faster rate after their invention than personal computers, television, radio, and indoor plumbing.

ers or hikers, and much more. What we've got now are tiny, programmable computers that also act as phones.

SO WHAT COULD POSSIBLY GO WRONG?

There are three broad areas of threat to cell phone users. First, there is the possibility that someone could listen in on your conversations or obtain a list of people you called or who called you. The second problem is that the more cell phones become tiny computers, the more likely they can become the target of viruses and spyware. And the third problem: If you put your whole life inside a little plastic box, what happens if it is stolen, lost, or damaged?

When the first cell phones were offered, many of them used analog technology; think of radio waves that warbled up and down or changed shape. Phones using that sort of system could be pretty easily listened in on by eavesdroppers with radio scanners; it's not legal, but that wouldn't stop someone from trying.

But today nearly all current cell companies have made the switch to digital, and if somehow you have held on to an analog phone, you are not likely to find many places where it can be used. Instead of sending radio waves, current cell phones broadcast and receive 0s and 1s in the same sort of code that is used by personal computers and by the Internet. There are clues that will tell you if your phone speaks digital: if it uses a SIM card for its identity, if it is capable of surfing the Web, if it can send and receive SMS text messages, or if it can send or receive video or pictures or music.

It is much more difficult for someone to eavesdrop on a digital phone; someone has to have your phone number as well as the unpublished serial number for the phone itself. Even with that information, the person would have to crack the code of the cell phone service. But it's not impossible.

Who could obtain this sort of information? The provider of your cell phone service knows it all. The government or the police could obtain it from your cell phone service if it obtained a court order. And an evildoer may be able to eavesdrop if you provide the information willingly or if you allow a virus to take control of your phone.

But there is one other way that someone could eavesdrop on at least one half of your conversation. Think about how many times you've been on a bus or in a restaurant or just walking down the hall and you've heard someone talking loudly into his or her phone. It's a strange world we live in, overhearing halves of conversations from strangers. How often have you heard something deeply personal float by your ear? Have you ever listened as someone placed an order using their credit card?

SIM City

A SIM card is a tiny piece of electronic memory that a digital phone uses to identify itself to the network. In some designs, it also holds your address book and things you have done to personalize your phone, like ringtones or pictures. SIM stands for Subscriber Identity Module.

If you are a baseball fan, watch carefully the next time the catcher trots out to the mound to have a quick strategy session with the pitcher about how to throw to the batter at the plate. Almost always the catcher leaves his mask on, and the pitcher holds his glove up to his face. Why? So that the batter and any opposing players cannot see their lips or overhear their conversation. Football quarterbacks use code words and numbers when they call plays.

Back to your cell phone, then. If you must discuss something personal or disclose information like your credit card or banking account number, stop and look around to see if anyone is within listening distance. Cup your phone in your hands or move away from others.

VIRUSES ON CELL PHONES

If you are using your cell phone like a computer—checking e-mail, surfing the Web, and downloading special programs to perform nifty new tasks—how, then, is it not a computer? And if we can agree that your small cell phone is actually a simplified version of a computer, then we can also agree that it is a tempting target for scam artists and nasty viruses. There have already been a number of attacks aimed at cell phones, and it is only a matter of time before evildoers shift some of their attention away from desktop and laptop PCs and toward phones.

The first mobile phone virus was discovered way back in 2004 and affected phones from companies including Nokia, Samsung, and Sony Ericsson; it spread from phone to phone using Bluetooth wireless communication.

As with your computer, never download files from people or places you don't know or trust. The most dangerous files are those that are intended to do something on your phone: Ringtones, games, and utility programs are at the top of that list.

Current cell phones have begun to come equipped with basic antivirus programs, and in theory the manufacturers and your cell phone company should keep the software up to date. If you use your cell phone on the Internet regularly, you may want to purchase and use an antivirus program designed to work on your phone.

Here are some of the things a cell phone virus could do:

1. Steal information stored on your phone, such as credit card numbers, bank account numbers, and the contents of your address book.
2. Use your phone account, without your knowledge or permission, to make expensive international calls.

3. Download a virus that can do the same sort of things that
   can occur on an infected computer, such as erasing files or
   causing unpredictable or unwanted behavior.

How do you avoid infecting your cell phone? Follow the same basic
rules of safety practices you do for your PC: Do not install software
from sources you do not know and trust; do not open attachments
that come to you as e-mail unless you know and trust the sender;
do not click on Web links in e-mail messages unless you are certain
they are legitimate. When in doubt, contact your cell phone service
provider and ask for advice.

Another way some cell phones can pick up a virus or spyware is
through a wireless connection. Some hackers program computers to
try to push infected software onto cell phones that are used in WiFi or
Bluetooth networks. For example, your phone may be able to switch
over from a distant cell phone tower to use the Internet in a cybercafé,
an office, or other location. When this happens, the phone becomes
just another device in the network, and you may find that you receive
a message about the installation of software you did not ask for.

For example, a message might read, "Would you like to install this
program now?" If your first response is, "What software?" your phone
is probably in danger. Try clicking on "no." If that doesn't work—and
sometimes evildoers try to force you to click "yes"—you can take your
phone out of the area. Bluetooth and WiFi networks generally only
work for a distance of 50 to 100 feet from the transmitter, and you can
break the connection by moving farther away. Or you could turn off
your phone until you are somewhere else.

Unless you plan to use Bluetooth or WiFi, you should turn off that
capability on your phone. (In addition to exposing you to the possibility of problems, it also uses battery power.) Ask your cell phone
company for assistance if you can't figure out how to set up your
device the way you want.

A LOST CAUSE

If the only copy of your important telephone address book is on your
cell phone, you are just begging for a problem sooner or later. Your
phone may be lost or stolen, it might break, or in certain unusual
circumstances it could lose its memory. Here are things you should
do to safeguard the information in your phone:

1. Make copies of all of your phone numbers and store the
   information somewhere else. If your phone permits, you

may be able to upload the contents of your phone book to your computer and keep a copy there; you should also make a printout of the address book and file it away in case the computer suffers a fate similar to that of your phone.

2. Consider buying a little notebook and making your own list of essential names and numbers. You will want to use something called a "pen" or a "pencil" and then apply it to "paper."

3. On your cell phone, make sure all of your phone book entries are saved to the SIM card; if your phone allows, have the numbers also saved to the built-in memory of your phone. Most SIM cards will hold about 250 names and phone numbers; some have a larger capacity. Saving the information to the SIM card allows you the chance to transfer it to a new phone if your old one dies or you decide to upgrade your equipment. Saving the numbers to your phone's built-in memory protects you in case the SIM card somehow becomes damaged.

4. Try to avoid subjecting your phone to situations in which it could be damaged. The biggest threats: water, extreme heat, and high levels of magnetism. So, don't drop your phone into the bathtub or swimming pool (or worse). Don't spill a cup of coffee on it, and don't leave it in a hot car or cook it in an oven.

   Avoid bringing the phone near something that has a strong magnet. (Where are there strong magnets? In big electric motors, in MRI machines in medical facilities, and in certain factories. This is not a common threat for most of us, but if there is a big sign on the wall saying "Dangerous magnetic energy," leave your cell phone somewhere else.)

5. Consider locking your cell phone with a password. It can be a pain in the neck to have to enter the code every time you turn on your phone, but it does offer some protection against a stranger reading your phone book or making unauthorized calls. Read the instruction manual (or call your cell phone provider) for advice on how to set up your phone for locking and unlocking. Some phones allow you to answer calls without unlocking; others automatically lock themselves after a specified period of time.

USING CALLER ID

One of the niceties of nearly all cells phone is that the service comes with caller ID: The name or the phone number of whoever is call-

If Your Phone Disappears

If you lose your phone and think it might have been left somewhere by accident, some people immediately try calling their number. If you're lucky, someone will answer the phone; if you're even luckier, that person will be honest and helpful and arrange to get the phone back to you. If the person asks to meet you or demands a ransom, be suspicious. Discuss the matter with a responsible adult.

If you believe your phone has been stolen, or you cannot find it, get to another phone and immediately call the cellular provider to notify them. The quicker you do that, the less chance that whoever has your phone will run up charges you may be asked to pay.

The phone company can electronically block the use of your missing phone. You will probably be able to keep your old phone number when you get a new phone.

Make sure you make notes about the date and time you make the call to the phone company. Ask for a confirmation number or the name and ID of the representative. Ask for confirmation by letter or e-mail that they have received your call.

If your phone was new and valuable, you may be able to file a claim with your insurance company. In order to do that, you should file a report with the police at the location where the phone was taken. (Some cell phone companies may require you to file the report so that you are off the hook if you dispute calls made by someone else.)

Finally, if your cell phone company gives you a hard time about removing unauthorized charges from your bill, call the phone company and request an investigation of your bill because your phone is being used by someone else. Then ask to speak to a supervisor and tell him or her that you will be filing a complaint with the Federal Communications Commission and your state attorney general if they do not remove the charges; that is usually enough to get them moving. Finally, file that complaint if you need to.

To reach the FCC, visit their Web site at www.fcc.gov/cgb/complaints.html or call them at (888) 225-5322.

ing appears on the screen. You can usually tell if the call is from a friend or a member of the family; you can often also tell if the call is from your boss or from a business or someone trying to sell you something.

You can choose to reject a call from someone with whom you don't want to speak; most phones allow you to do this by merely pressing the hang-up button without you ever having to actually answer the call. If someone you don't want to speak with repeatedly calls, you can save the incoming number to your phone book and identify it with a name like "reject this call."

There is a loophole, though. Some callers set up their phone number to block caller ID; their incoming calls may show up on your screen as "anonymous." You can still choose to reject the call, but then again it might be someone with whom you actually want to speak.

Some cell phone companies allow you to block specific telephone numbers so that they cannot be used to call you. This is not quite the same as being able to block a particular person from calling you because that person could always find another phone number from which to call.

One more thing: If someone calls you and threatens you in any way, speak to a trusted adult or call the police and discuss the matter.

BLOCK THAT CALL

We know callers can make their phone number anonymous when they call you. In some situations, and with certain cell phone companies, you can do the same. You might want to use this if you are calling a business and don't want them to record your number for their own purposes.

Some cell phones have a menu item that allows you to "hide ID" for the next call you make.

You may also be able to block caller ID of your number for the next call you make by pushing a few extra buttons. Try the following: *67 followed by the number you want to call. For example, *67555-555-5555.

Some cell phone companies permit this, while others do not. You can test this by calling someone you know and asking if your name or phone number came up on his or her screen. You can also check with your cell phone company to see if they use a different process.

Note that you cannot block identification of your number when calling emergency services like the police or fire departments and most government agencies. It may also not work on certain toll-free calling services.

PROTECTING YOUR ADDRESS BOOK

How would you feel about some stranger getting hold of a neatly organized list of the names of your best friends and your family?

Obviously, if your phone is stolen or lost, you should immediately contact the cell phone company and have them block service. But sometimes thieves are much quicker to act than their victims. Imagine this: Someone steals your phone and wallet and then quickly sends a text message to your mother asking her to send you back a message reminding you of your ATM pin.

One safeguard is to password-protect your phone so that no one can use it without the code. (Make sure you apply the password to both the phone itself and to the SIM card that is held within.) If you need assistance on putting a password on your phone, call the help desk at your cell phone company.

Although it may look very professional to identify the people in your address book by their full name, it might make more sense to use nicknames to protect them from snoops. Just make sure you use IDs that you'll remember.

You probably shouldn't list your PIN codes in the phone, but if you do make sure they are not directly associated with the ATM or debit card they unlock. You could hide the pin code in a made-up telephone listing in your address book; for example, make up an entry for Debbie Cardozo as a stand-in for Debit Card.

DEALING WITH SUSPICIOUS MESSAGES

In general, you should always assume that any text message, e-mail, or phone call you receive that asks for personal or financial information is a fraud. A bank or a credit card company is not going to ask you to tell them your account number; they already know it.

If you have called a reputable company or contacted them over the Internet to buy something, you are going to have to provide your card number and your address. But at least you know that you made the call.

But if you receive a message asking you to "verify," "update," or otherwise provide your private information, STOP. Your best step would be to call the bank or credit card company or whatever is the supposed source of the request. Do not use the telephone number or e-mail address that might appear in the message; the thieves could easily answer the phone using a name that sounds legitimate. Instead, find the number to call by looking at the back of your bank card or by going to a bank branch.

A Secret Decoder Ring

One thing you should not put on your cell phone: your passwords and important information like credit cards or banking account numbers in a form that a stranger might be able to read. Instead, keep the phone number for the credit card company and just the last four digits of the card, like this: 3416. If you are traveling far from home, you might keep a copy of the same information on an index card in your pocket and in your suitcase.

That's all you need to know in order to call the company and tell them your wallet has been stolen or lost. After you call the bank or credit card company, they will ask questions designed to prove who you are; that's a good thing. If you put any more detail on your phone or on your reminder card, you're giving a thief the information needed to go on a spending spree.

Sometimes, though, you might use a secret code. It doesn't have to be that complex—just confusing enough to slow down a thief and give you enough time to call and cancel your cards and phone service. How about swapping the first three digits of your credit card with the last three digits? Let's say your number is 7894-123-8904. With a swap, the number becomes 9044-123-8789. You can make up any variation that makes sense to you; how about pulling the middle three digits and writing them down in reverse order at the start of the number? Whatever you do, make sure you memorize the trick and then you can write down the coded number.

Also keep the emergency notification number for the cell phone company on a separate piece of paper so that you can call them if your phone is missing. Otherwise, you just might end up responsible for calls made by a thief.

If someone is badgering you or threatening you, tell a responsible adult or contact the police. A threat—even if it is delivered in an electronic form rather than directly to your face—is still a serious matter.

Coming to the world of scams, do you really think that someone out there is going to contact you out of the blue and announce that you are the winner of a huge lottery you never entered? Or is it reasonable to believe that someone would offer you $500 more than the price you have listed on an online Web site where you are trying to sell your used bicycle? If it seems too good to be true—it almost always is.

YOUR PRIVATE PICTURES

Just as with your Facebook or other social networking page, do not assume that any photos you take with your cell phone camera could not somehow end up being seen by other people without your permission.

First, if your phone is lost or stolen (and the phone and its SIM are not protected by a password) anyone can look at your pictures. Second, if you send the pictures to someone by e-mail from your phone, they are out of your control; whomever you send them to might send them to someone else on purpose or by accident. Finally, think twice before uploading highly personal photos to one of the online storage sites offered by some cell phone companies. It may be fun and convenient to send your pictures to a repository at T-Mobile or Sprint or whichever company you use; it might also be fun to allow your friends to sign on to that site and use the password you provide them so that they can look at the pictures. But do not overlook the possibility that the pictures and other information will not somehow break loose. It happened to a semifamous celebrity whose first name is the same as the capital city of France.

REVIEW YOUR BILL

One of the easiest ways to spot a problem with your cell phone account is to actually read the bill when it comes in each month. Even if your parents are paying the bill . . . ask to see it. You not only might help save the family from being ripped off, but you may be able to spot a security lapse on your own phone.

Here is what to look for:

▸ Calls to people or phone numbers you don't recognize, or to foreign locations you know you did not call.
▸ Calls made at odd times of the day or night. If you're always asleep at 3 A.M. on weekdays, there shouldn't be any charges for *outgoing* calls or text messages at that time; remember, though, that most cell phone plans make you pay for calls or messages you receive, even if they are sent to a sleeping phone.
▸ Charges for services you did not use, such as ringtones, games, directory assistance, or anything else.

When in doubt, call your cell phone company and ask them to explain your bill and justify any charges that seem incorrect. Don't be afraid to speak up if you think someone has gotten hold of your account or is otherwise scamming you (or your parents.)

SPAM BY TEXT MESSAGE

One of the most annoying things about owning a cell phone is finding that telemarketers or spammers have obtained your phone number or your text message address (which is often related to your phone number.) The next thing that happens is that you begin to receive calls or text messages trying to sell you all sorts of things you don't want to buy. And even worse, under most plans you have to pay for the incoming call or message.

Although the federal government does maintain a "do not call" service intended to prevent telemarketers from bothering you if you list your number there, that is of no use against many spammers who operate from a foreign location.

You can begin your defense by being very careful about who you give your cell phone number to. And if the problem becomes severe, contact your cell phone provider and ask about services they offer to block certain callers or messages and about spam-filtering services they can apply to eliminate waves of messages sent to their subscribers. If your phone begins to fill up with junk after you have contacted the cell phone company, don't be shy about insisting on a refund of charges.

TELEPHONE FRAUD

When someone you don't know calls and tries to sell you something or ask you for personal information, keep your cool and slow things down immediately. You might politely but firmly interrupt and ask: "Are you trying to sell me something?" Then listen carefully for just a moment. If you don't like what you hear, grab a pen and piece of paper and ask the following three questions:

1. Can I have your name and the name of your company, please? Could you spell that for me, please.
2. What is your telephone number?
3. I want you to remove my name and telephone number from your call list, and I do not want you to call me again. Do you understand?

Then hang up the phone.

Dumping Your Old Cell Phone Safely

We live in a world of disposable items. The only thing worth replacing on your cell phone is its battery if it loses its ability to hold a charge. Other than that, they're not meant to be repaired if something breaks.

Very often a cell phone is retired while it is still in working condition. For example, you may have decided to upgrade to the latest and greatest toy for its fantastic new features or because you want to choose a color to match your new shoes.

The first thing you should do is remove all personal information from the phone's built-in memory. Erase all phone numbers, messages, call histories, passwords, pictures, notes . . . anything that's on the phone. If you need help in doing this, consult your cell phone company's technical support staff.

(The information on the phone's SIM card may have moved to your new phone; if the card is still in place, remove it from the phone.)

You might choose to hold on to your old phone to serve as a backup just in case your new one is lost, stolen, or breaks. In that situation, you should remove the battery from your old phone (just in case it leaks) and then store the phone, the battery, and its charger in a dry place away from heat.

If you have no need for the old phone, consider donating it to charities that recycle the devices as emergency phones or for use in third-world countries. Your cell phone company should be able to give you advice here.

Or you can try to sell your old phone. In order for someone to use your old phone they will either have to use the same cell phone company as you do, or you will need to "unlock" your phone so that it is not tied to one provider. Some cell phone companies will give you the secret codes for unlocking the phone; in other cases, you may have to surf the Internet to find someone who will do the service for you for a fee.

What should you do if your phone is broken? You need to recycle carefully. Remove the battery and the SIM card. Then check with your local government or trash company about how they recommend disposing of the parts. The battery, for example, usually contains heavy metals that can be dangerous if not disposed of properly.

Who's Calling, Please?

Some disreputable companies and most crooks will try to block the display of their information when they call. If you see "anonymous" or some obviously phony phone number like 000-000-0000 on the caller ID, that's often enough to refuse to take the call on your cell phone.

It may be true that some phone calls from strangers are legitimate. You might have even requested a call (or given permission to be called) when you visited a particular Web site or entered a contest or inquired about a product.

But the tipoff that the call may be something you don't want is in the tone of the caller. Is he or she trying to push you? Is the person trying to convince you that there is a real rush to do something? What is the response if you ask for something in writing by mail or by e-mail? A legitimate business should always be willing to send you terms and conditions in writing, or at the very least point you to a page on the Internet that includes that information and which allows you to print out or save a copy in case there is a later dispute over who said what.

One way to address any sales situation is this: If someone starts to talk very quickly, you respond very slowly. This way you cannot be pushed or rushed into making a decision.

TELEPHONE FRAUD WARNING SIGNS

If someone is offering you a "free" anything, make sure there are no service charges or shipping fees or any other strings attached. Free means free; if someone offers you a $10 case for your cell phone for free but there is a $14.99 charge for shipping and handling, the person is selling you a $10 case for $14.99. That's a bad deal.

The same goes for prizes and lotteries and other things someone might declare to be coming your way. If it's a prize, there shouldn't be any fees attached to it.

Another sign of fraud is if a caller asks you to confirm your account information at a bank, credit card company, or an online store. If you have given Amazon or eBay or any other Internet retailer your information in the past, they have it; they will not ask you to confirm it on the phone or by e-mail. If you give your information to a caller, it will likely be used to charge you for a purchase or steal from your accounts.

If people make this kind of call, ask for their name, the company they work for, and phone number; tell them you will call them back. If you know the company, find their telephone number on a statement or their official Web page and ask to speak with customer service; discuss the call you have received and ask them to tell you their policies.

If you have any suspicions at all about the caller or the company, don't do any business with them.

PUTTING THE LAW ON YOUR SIDE

Under federal law, you have a number of rights intended to protect you against telemarketers. You can list your telephone number on a national "Do not call" list; it's not perfect—some companies intentionally or accidentally make calls when they should not, and crooks pay it no attention at all. Callers from outside the United States routinely ignore the law. But putting your home or cell phone number (or both) on the list will definitely reduce the number of telemarketing calls you receive.

Here's how to sign up: Go to the Web site DoNotCall.gov and fill out the form there. You can also register by phone by calling (888) 382-1222 from the number you want to put on the list. If you register online, it is a two-part process. First you register, and then you must click on the confirmation e-mail you will receive.

Under a revision of the law that took effect in 2008, you do not need to renew your listing every few years; your number will remain on the list until and unless you take it off or your number is disconnected and reassigned to someone else. Read the instructions to learn about your rights and how to verify that your number is properly registered.

There are a few problems, however. If you give a company permission to call you, they can do so even if your number is on the list; make sure to pay attention when you fill out any contest forms or open an account online. Look for little check boxes that give the company the right to call you and uncheck them if you don't want to be bothered.

The law also does not affect political candidates, charities, and government agencies and does not protect you if your phone is listed in the name of a company and not a person. Companies that you do business with—and that have your number—may call for 18 months. If you ask a company for information, it may call for three months.

Whether your number is on the list or not, telemarketers are not supposed to call you at all between the hours of 9 P.M. and 8 A.M. the next morning. If someone does call, ask for a name and number and write it down.

CALLING IN THE FEDS

Earlier in this section, you learned to get the name of anyone calling you, their company name, and their phone number before telling them not to call you again. If you tell them not to call you and to put your number on their do-not-call list, they are breaking the law if they call again.

You can learn a bit more about how some phone scams work by reading a Web page of the Federal Trade Commission at www.ftc. gov/phonefraud.

To report an actual instance of phone fraud, follow the links from the FTC's home page at www.FTC.gov or call (877) FTC-HELP.

To report violations of the National Do Not Call Registry, visit www.DoNotCall.gov or call (888) 382-1222.

Complaints that are reported to the FTC are made part of something called the Consumer Sentinel Network, a database that is available to law-enforcement agencies around the world. The more information they get, the better their chances to find patterns and new scams and scammers.

TEXT MESSAGE SCAMS

Another scam involves receiving a text message on your cell phone from someone you don't know who is warning you about something that has nothing to do with you. The most common is a message claiming to be from a bank or a credit card company, asking you to call to "verify" your information.

If the bank was really in need of checking with you, they could call you on the phone. It makes no sense for a company that should already have your information (if you have an account with them) to ask you to verify or supply it again.

If you receive a message like this, here's what should you do:

1. If the message is obviously a fraud—for example, from a bank or credit card company where you do not have an account, do not respond in any way.

2. If somehow, probably entirely by accident, you do have an account with the company named in the message, find the customer service number and call directly. Do not use the phone number in the text message or any Web site it might list. You can get the correct phone number from the back of your credit or debit card or from a printed phone book or bank statement. Be prepared to read the message to the customer service representative.

3. Then call your cell phone company and ask them how they plan to protect you from this sort of fraud. Can they block incoming text messages? Do they offer a service (called a "whitelist") that allows only senders you put on the list to send you a message? Finally, will they give you a credit on your bill for spam and scam messages?

There are other types of rip-offs that come through your cell phone. Be very careful about revealing your cell phone number on any Web site you visit, especially those that offer to send games or horoscopes

Phishing by Phone

Here's a true story of a cell phone user who received a text message claiming to be from a federal credit union in San Francisco. The message read: "You need to verify your Embarcadero FCU acct | unusual activity |, call at 8005xx-xxxx"

In a posting on a blog, the cell phone user told his story: "I was wary at first and I looked up Embarcadero FCU on Google and it pretty much pointed to the Embarcadero Federal Credit Union Web site. The numbers didn't match for the contact and when I did call the number listed in the text, it sounded fishy asking for 3 forms of ID including my credit card number. I hung up at that point."

The only thing wrong here is that the person who got the message actually called the phone number. There is no reason to make the call, and in doing so he revealed his phone number to the scammer. He probably made it almost certain that future calls and messages will come to his phone.

or sports scores to your phone. Some of these sites are trying to get you to agree to their service without reading the tiny print on the page that tells you of a daily or monthly charge.

If you receive a bill with unexpected charges, immediately call the customer service department for your cell phone company and seek their assistance. They should be able to help you get in touch with the service that is charging you the fee, and they may be willing to give you credit for some or all of the charges.

The quicker you contact the cell phone company, they better the chance that they will help you. And if they don't offer to help, find out how long you have left on your contract with the cell phone company; you may be surprised to see how suddenly cooperative they may become if you threaten to switch brands.

WHAT YOU NEED TO KNOW

> The most current cell phones are much more than portable telephones. They can also access the Internet and send and receive e-mail, video, music, and messages.

> The more computer functions that are squeezed into a cell phone, the more care you must take to avoid viruses and scams. Don't do anything on an Internet-connected phone you wouldn't (or shouldn't) do on a computer.

> Don't let your cell phone or portable digital device hold the only copy of your phone and address book. If your phone is lost, stolen, or damaged, you will lose access to the list.

> Never store important personal information such as your full credit, debit, or bank account numbers on your cell phone. There are, though, some codes and tricks you can use to help protect you in case your phone or your wallet goes missing.

> Take care with any photos, videos, or personal messages on your phone. Don't assume they cannot be misused by other people.

> Learn how to use local and federal agencies and law enforcement to protect yourself from theft and scams.

13 ▮▮

Wireless Security

When you connect wirelessly to the Internet with your laptop, iPhone, or other device, you are basically using it to shout across the room. Everything you send or receive is carried on a radio wave that can be picked up not just by your electronic device but by any other receiver within range. Think of your cell phone or your laptop as a radio transmitter and receiver that can be moved from place to place to find different systems to communicate with.

The good news, though, is that most electronic devices are designed so that although their signals can be picked up quite easily, most of the information that is sent back and forth is sent in code. It's called encryption.

The more current your device, the more likely it has a good system to encrypt the data. You should consult with the manufacturer or the help desk of your Internet or cell service provider for assistance in making choices when you first start using your device or if you install a WiFi system in your home.

JUST A BIT OF TECHNOBABBLE

The device that connects to the Internet is called a router (*ou* is pronounced like *ouch*). There are routers at public sites, and if you install a wireless system in your home, you'll have your own.

Here are some more technical details to keep in mind:

1. If you have a choice of types of encryption, WiFi Protected Access (WPA) is stronger than Wired Equivalent Privacy

(WEP). Both ends of the connection—the receiver and the transmitter—need to be able to use the same system, but that is usually not a problem since routers can switch back and forth between WPA and WEP.

2. Oddly enough, many routers you might buy for use in your home come with encryption turned off. Make sure you turn it on.

3. Make sure your laptop has a current copy of antivirus and antispyware software installed, as well as a firewall to block unwanted intruders.

4. If you install a wireless router in your home, make sure that you change its standard (called default) name and password to ones that you choose. As an example, most routers from Linksys—just one of a number of manufacturers—are set up with the clever name of "Linksys" and also with a common password; if you don't change them, one of your neighbors or a passerby might be able to "see" your network and come right in. At the very least, they would be able to use your WiFi system to get on the Internet. If you also have set up your computers so that anyone on your network can read or move files from place to place, you will also be opening up that information to an intruder.

5. If you've got a broadband network attached to your wireless network (a cable or DSL modem are the most common) you might want to turn off your wireless network when you're not using it. And you certainly do not want to leave your computers on and connected to the Internet all the time unless you have a firewall in place.

6. Even with all of these safety tips, you should always assume that any time you connect to a public WiFi network (at an Internet café or a library, for example) your communication may be intercepted. It's okay to do research on the Web, and probably okay to send and receive e-mail. However, you probably don't want to pay bills or do your banking from a public site. If you absolutely must conduct business in a place where you are not certain of the security, be sure to change your passwords frequently.

USING A PUBLIC COMPUTER

One of the most dangerous places to do any serious computing is at a public machine at an Internet café, a library, or a school. You have no way of knowing if some evildoer has planted a keylogger or some other hidden program that can capture your user names and passwords.

Keep your use of a public computer to matters that are not private. For example, you can do research on a search engine (google.com or live.com, for example) without having to supply any personal information. You can check the weather or train schedules or visit your favorite celebrity Web site without concern.

But if it is important to go to a site where you must enter a user name and password, there are a few things you can do to make it less likely that someone can come along later and learn some of your secrets:

1. Bring your own browser. For example, you can install a portable version of the Firefox browser on a flash memory

Secure Wireless Computing

If you're at an Internet café or other public wireless site and using your own laptop, the safest way to protect your online credit or debit card or banking account is to *stay away from those Web sites.* The same is also true of shopping sites where you need to enter card or account numbers. You're better off if you can wait until you are back home or at a site you know to be protected against snoops.

However, if you must do some business using your laptop or other WiFi device, make sure you use secure or encrypted sites. These are Web pages that are designed to make it very difficult for an outsider to see anything you transmit or receive.

When you go to a bank or credit or debit card site or to the "shopping cart" or "checkout" of an online store, make sure you see an extra "s" as in *secure* in the "http" part of the Web address. For example, https://www.bankofeastovershoe.com.

If you see the "s" in the address, anyone trying to electronically eavesdrop on the connection between your laptop and the Internet will only be able to see a very difficult to break encrypted (that means hidden in a code) signal. If the "s" goes away at any point while you are conducting business, stop what you are doing and sign off.

key that you plug into the public computer. This way you know that the browser does not contain any hidden snoops.

2. Use the bookmarks on your browser to go to Web sites instead of typing them in. This makes it impossible for a keylogger that might be on the public computer to know where you have gone.

3. Close the browser when you are done so that the next person cannot come along and read your history of sites visited.

4. The next time you are back home or at a place where you trust the security of the machine you are using, change the passwords for any Web site you visited while you were using the public machine.

To obtain a free copy of a portable version of Firefox, visit http://portableapps.com/apps/internet/firefox_portable

WHAT YOU NEED TO KNOW

> Using your laptop or cell phone for wireless connection to the Internet is convenient and fun. It is also—depending on the equipment you use and the location where you use it—possibly a threat to your privacy and the security of any financial transactions you make.

> There are steps you can take to enhance the security of a WiFi system you use in your home.

> If you are using a computer in an Internet café or at a library, school, or other public location, you should be very careful about the sort of information you transmit, and you should plan on changing passwords frequently.

14

How to Help Friends Cope with Internet and Online Dangers

What would you do if one of your friends was in danger? If you're a true friend, the answer shouldn't take much thought: You'd try to help.

So let's begin with the recognition that dangers that exist on the Internet can really threaten your friend's personal safety, his or her health, or seriously damage reputations, college applications, or job prospects. You're off to a great start by reading this book, which should help you understand the threats.

Then do what friends do: Talk about the things you see going on. If someone has begun to drop out of the real world and descend into near full-time existence in the virtual world, talk about it. Try to get your friend involved in activities that don't require a computer or a cell phone.

If your friend seems ready to visit with someone from an online "meeting," ask about what considerations he or she has given to personal safety. Share the ideas included in this book: involving an adult or a trusted friend as a buddy, sharing all of the details about a meeting with a stranger, arranging for a cell phone "check-in" during a date, and doing all of the other things that allow a young person to maintain some control over an encounter.

Tell your friend about ways you have learned to establish a personal safety net for everything you do on the Internet. It all begins with ending the secrecy and sharing your life with someone you trust.

IS SOMEONE YOU CARE ABOUT ADDICTED TO THE NET?

It really doesn't require a doctor to diagnose someone who has developed an addiction to the Internet or who has begun to engage in dangerous activity in the virtual world. It merely needs someone who cares . . . and someone who can get past the walls some of us erect around our inner feelings and what we think of as our private behavior.

Go back to chapter 1 of this book and reread the Internet Addiction Test included there. This self-examination, developed by the Center for Internet Addiction Recovery, asks questions of individuals about their behavior. When you read it again, answer the questions as if you were your friend.

Is your friend dropping back into cyberspace and shutting out friends? Are his or her grades or schoolwork suffering because of the amount of time spent online? Is someone you know covering up a secret life devoted to things found on the Internet such as gambling, pornography, social chat rooms, or is the friend getting into serious debt?

When you're finished filling in the survey about your friend, ask yourself one more question: If you don't help your friend, who will?

INVOLVING OTHERS

Only you know exactly how close you are to a person and where the lines and boundaries of that relationship begin and end. Consider, though, whether you can and should involve some other friends in a show of support. In treatment of other disorders, including addiction to drugs or gambling, this is often called an "intervention." People who love or care about someone else get together to give that person the straight news.

You might also ask a school guidance counselor or a medical professional for some suggestions about how to help your friend break away from an Internet addiction or change his or her habits to be safer. They may have suggestions about local support groups or clubs that might be helpful.

WHAT YOU NEED TO KNOW

> ▶ If someone you know and care about is becoming detached from the real world, consider what you can do to help. Talk

to your friend about your concern. Involve him or her in activities away from the Internet and other forms of electronic communication.

▶ Don't be judgmental of another person. Express your feelings and your concern and offer your help. Sometimes you just need to offer someone your ear instead of your voice: Listen to what's on his or her mind.

▶ Share the safety and security tips you've read about in this book. Discuss the dangers and the positive suggestions as well.

▶ If you believe a friend or family member is in immediate personal danger, do not wait. Contact a responsible adult or the police.

GLOSSARY

This glossary defines many of the terms about the online world included in this book and adds some specific warnings to protect your personal safety and privacy.

address   The location, in cyberspace, of a particular Web site. When you enter an address or click on its name in a browser or e-mail, your computer communicates over the Internet with a directory that gives it instructions on how to make contact with and display the Web site. *See also* **URL.**

adware   A form of **malware** that infects a computer with links to advertising—often in the form of pop-up ads—that may slow down or interfere with your use of the machine. Many **antivirus** or **Internet security programs** can block installation of adware or remove it from an already infected computer.

antivirus   A specialized piece of software that is intended to block the download of a **virus** to your computer or other electronic device, or to recognize that some form of **malware** has somehow gotten through and prevented it from causing damage to your files.

applications   **Software** or computer code designed to perform a specific task such as word processing, Web browsing, or digital editing and playback of music or video. A computer also needs an **operating system** to manage the connection between applications and the **hardware** of the machine itself.

attachment   A file of any sort, including text, music, photos, video, or a program that is included along with an e-mail communication. If you know and trust the sender—and have a capable and up-to-date **antivirus** program installed on your system—you can accept an attachment. If you do not know the sender or expect an attachment, it may be wise to delete the e-mail without opening it.

blacklisting   A type of filter that can be used to block access to certain Web sites or turn away certain e-mails. Web or e-mail addresses included on the blacklist are rejected. This form of filter does not examine content of sites or mail. *See also* **whitelisting**.

blog   A web log or journal. The original idea of a blog was for personal or noncommercial diaries or observations, usually organized by date. Today, blogs are also found on news and opinion Web sites, pages promoting politicians, entertainers, and athletes, and on commercial sites. If you post (upload) some writing to your own blog or someone else's blog, you should always remember that once something is on the Internet it may be impossible to completely remove it. For that reason, you should be very careful not to post something that might embarrass you now or years from now.

botnet   *See* **bots**.

bots   Computers that have been infected with a program that makes them perform tasks like sending out e-mail spam without the owner's knowledge or permission. An individual computer may be made part of a group of bots, called a **botnet.** Many **antivirus** or **Internet security programs** can block installation of bot infections or remove them from an already infected computer.

browser   A program that allows you to go to various locations on the Internet and interact with the Web sites you find. Examples include Microsoft Internet Explorer, Mozilla Firefox, and Google Chrome.

browser highjacking   A scheme by hijackers operating on the Net to send your **browser** to a Web site other than the one you have requested. The act of hijacking a browser for the purpose of obtaining information is sometimes called pharming (*see* **browser highjacking**). Current versions of browsers, including major browsers, are supposed to be able to alert you if you have been sent to a Web site intended for **phishing** information from your machine, or if the Web site you are viewing has some contradiction between what it claims to be and the way it is registered with the keepers of the Internet.

browsing   The act of searching for a particular bit of information or a Web site on the Internet. An Internet **browser** allows you to enter a Web address or to go to a **search engine** page to find what you are looking for. Browsing is also called **navigating** or **surfing.**

bulletin boards   An electronic form of a corkboard where individuals can post messages or news. Some bulletin boards require members to register, while others are open to anyone who views the page. Some boards are "moderated," meaning that there is someone who is supposed to oversee the content of the postings and in most arrangements remove anything that is inappropriate or offensive.

chat   Real-time communication over the Internet, also known as instant messaging (*see* **IM**). Users enter text in a box on their computer screen and then send the message to someone using the same messaging service or participating in a chat room on a social networking Web site. Communication is nearly instant when both parties are signed on at the same time.

chat room   A location on a Web site where two or more users can exchange messages with one another. Some chat rooms are open to anyone who chooses to join in, while others are limited to those who are invited to join by one or more participants. A relatively few chat rooms are monitored, meaning that someone oversees the content of the messages that are exchanged and can block someone from membership; other systems encourage users to report anyone who engages in offensive or inappropriate behavior.

cookie   A small bit of code that is installed on your computer by certain Web sites. They may help identify you to the Web site as a previous visitor, which may be harmless. Or they may be used by the Web site operator to track your visits. You can adjust settings in your **browser** to allow or not allow installation of cookies, although some Web sites will not allow you to visit without the cookies setting turned on. You can also make settings on your browser or security software to erase all cookies saved on your computer as part of its shutdown process. *See also* **temporary files.**

cyberbullying   Using the Internet, cell phones, or other digital communication devices to send or post messages or images intended to harm people or force them to do something they don't want to do. Also includes posting slanderous or hurtful messages or profiles about someone.

cyberspace   A general name for the imaginary place where electronic communication and commerce occurs. The term includes the Internet as well as other technologies. One way to think of where cyberspace is: When you are on the phone with someone, the back-and-forth of your conversation is not on your phone or the person with whom you are talking, but instead in cyberspace.

cyberstalking   Using the Internet, cell phones, or other communication devices to spy on the activities of others or to attempt to lure a child or an adult to travel or perform an activity.

Also to repeatedly send messages to someone who does not want to receive them.

discussion group An online gathering of people with common interests or a desire to exchange information about a particular subject.

domain name The label used as a substitute for the computer's numerical address for a Web site. Web browsers go to a Domain Name Service index on the Internet and swap the domain name for the complex numerical or Internet Protocol (IP) address of a Web site. As an example, Amazon.com is a domain name and one of its IP addresses is 72.21.203.1.

download Transferring files or software from another user or from a location on the Internet or from CDs or DVDs to your computer. If you send files to another user or location, it is an upload.

e-mail Short for electronic mail, this is a service that permits people to send messages from their computer or other electronic device such as a cell phone to another computer or device. The sender and the receiver do not need to be online at the same time. The e-mail service will store the message and deliver it when the other person signs on. This is different from an instant message (**IM**) service, which requires both parties to be connected to the Internet and signed on to the program in order to zap messages back and forth.

emoticons Facelike icons, sometimes animated, that can be used to show emotions (happy, sad, angry, bored) in e-mails, chat, and instant messaging.

encryption Scrambling or encoding of data so that only devices that are properly set up can read and use the information. Most wireless routers, laptops, and Internet-capable cell phones can be set up to use encryption.

extortionware A form of **malware** (not very common) that encrypts or hides important personal files, demanding payment of money to unlock the data. Using an **antivirus** program should protect against most such infections. *Contact police or other legal authorities for assistance in dealing with this sort of criminal activity.*

file-sharing programs A Web site or computer set up to allow many users to access or **download** the same file. A file-sharing site may be used to distribute music, videos, or software and may violate copyrights on the material. Files shared in this way may also be infected with viruses and other **malware.**

filter A program or a feature of a **browser** or Web site that allows someone to block access to certain pages or certain types of content that they find inappropriate. Parents can install a filter to block access to objectionable material. Teens can have their own filter to block mail or sites they don't want. Filters can **blacklist** an e-mail address or a Web site to block it, or **whitelist** it to specifically allow it. Some filters can also be set to block material containing specific words or words of a certain type.

firewall   A piece of electronic hardware or a software program that is intended to prevent **hackers** from breaking into your computer or Web sites from downloading **malware.** A properly installed firewall should prevent most attacks. However, it will not guard against viruses and other malware if you choose to "allow" a file to come in when the firewall issues a warning. Think of the firewall as existing outside of your computer; you should also have an up-to-date **antivirus** program on the inside of the wall to stop most malware that somehow manages to get through to your computer.

flaming   In a **chat room** or on a social network, sending an insulting, profane, or deliberately confrontational message to another person.

Flash   Macromedia's Flash is a utility that works with your Internet **browser** to allow it to display many types of animated content from a Web site. Because this is "active" material that causes your computer to perform functions by itself, you should have a capable **antivirus** program in place to guard against attempts to plant **malware** within Flash material.

hacker   Someone who wants to break into a network or an individual computer, or who tries to change a piece of **software** to do something other than what it was intended for. Most of the original hackers did it for fun; today, most are out to rip people off or cause damage.

hardware   The physical parts of a computer, including the keyboard, the hard drive, the motherboard that holds the microprocessor, memory, and the LCD or display. Other essential parts of the computer include its **operating system** and **applications.**

history   Nearly all Internet **browsers** maintain a list of sites you have visited. You can make settings to keep the history for the past day, week, month, or a longer period. Keeping the history makes it easier for you to find a site you visited in the past, but also makes it possible for an outsider to see where you have gone. Some safety programs used by parents makes copies of your browsing history. As a user you can instruct your browser to delete all records of your history each time you shut down the browser or turn off your computer.

home page   The Web page your Internet **browser** will display when it first is connected, or any time it is asked to return to "home." You can set the home page to any site you choose. Consult the help pages of your browser for instructions on how to do this.

HTML   The Hypertext Markup Language is the computer code or language used to create nearly all documents on the Web. As a user, you do not need to understand the coding; it is translated for you by your Web **browser.**

http   The Hypertext Transfer Protocol or http was the original design used in linking sites and pages on the Internet. Today, nearly all exchanges on the Web use http, and it is no longer necessary as part of a **URL** you enter into a modern **browser.** *See also* **URL.** A much less common protocol, used to directly connect one machine to another, is **ftp** or File Transfer Protocol.

https   A secure version of **http** used for transactions such as banking, credit or debit card accounts, or online shopping. A Web connection using https sends encrypted (or coded) information in both directions between your computer and the Web site.

hyperlinks   *See* **links.**

icon   A small drawing or piece of art that represents the programs, a folder, or an individual file on your computer.

ICQ   A version of an instant messaging program that allows users to communicate with each other in **real time.** Users can be alerted when certain other users log on to the program. It is pronounced "I seek you."

IM   An instant message or instant messaging service. This sort of service allows people to connect to one another in **real time** and send and receive messages almost instantly. Users need to have a copy of the instant messaging program on their computer, cell phone, or other electronic device and need to know the IM address of the person you want to exchange messages with.

inbox   On an e-mail system, the folder that holds e-mail you have received or the list of e-mail that is available on the central server waiting for you to download it to your computer or other electronic device.

instant messaging   *See* **IM.**

Internet   An interconnected network of computers around the world that allows the interchange of information by e-mail and the ability to visit Web sites maintained by companies, government agencies, schools, associations, and individuals.

Intranet   A private network that is set up within an organization (a school or a company, for example) to allow common access to information. By definition, there is little or limited access to an Intranet from the outside, such as over the Internet.

ISP (Internet Service Provider) A company or service that provides access to the Internet for individual users or groups of users. Most ISPs charge a monthly or annual fee, and offer connection by dial-up (telephone), broadband (cable television or DSL), or wireless (WiFi or other forms of radio service.)

Java A computer language used by some designers to create small applications or programs that can be run on a Web page. For example, a Web site might include a calculator that is "interactive" with you, allowing you to enter numbers or other information and receive an answer.

junk e-mail *See* **spam.**

keylogger **Malware** that makes records of **user names,** log-in names, **passwords,** and bank or credit card numbers as they are typed in from the keyboard. The owner of the keylogger may instruct it to send collected information over the Internet. If you use a public computer at an Internet café or a library or borrow someone's machine, you run the risk that the computer has a keylogger in place; for that reason, you might not want to visit any sites that require you to enter your password when you are away from your own machine.

keyword A term or phrase entered into a **search engine** to locate information or a Web site on the Internet. For example, to learn about security programs for your computer you could type "antivirus software" into the search box of a site like www. google.com or www.live.com or any of dozens of other search engines. Putting a two-or-more-word phrase within quotes tells the engine to search for that exact phrase; if you do not put the phrase in quotes, the engine will find Web sites that that have the words you have entered but not necessarily as a phrase.

link A connection from one Web site to another, or from an e-mail to a Web site. Clicking on an image or a portion of text sends the user to an identified location on the Web. Most links are harmless and are important parts of the interconnected sites that we call the Web. Some links, though, may go to sites displaying inappropriate material or to sites that may attempt to **download** a **virus** or other **malware.** The original name for links was hyperlinks, and you may see that term used in some places.

malware The general term for any piece of **software** written with the intent of damaging files, taking over control of a machine without permission, or stealing information. Malware includes **adware, keyloggers,** and **viruses.**

man-in-the-middle attack   A form of electronic eavesdropping in which someone uses a computer to intercept communication in a WiFi zone. One way this can be accomplished is to install an unauthorized **router** that acts as if it were the official receiver in a network and fooling users into connecting to it.

modem   An essential device in connecting your computer to the Internet. A modem (short of modulator-demodulator) converts between the 0s and 1s that your computer uses to handle data into a form that can be transmitted. There are modems that connect to telephone lines, cable television wires, and other forms of communication. If your laptop or cell phone connects wirelessly to the Internet, there is still the equivalent of a modem in the **hardware** to translate between differing technical languages.

mouse trapping   A technique by designers of some Web sites— often including pornography, gambling, or other pages—to lock a user in place. When you visit the site by entering its name in your Web **browser** or by clicking on a **link,** your screen may fill with many copies of the Web page, or you may find that you cannot navigate away from the page by trying to back out or enter a new address. Sometimes you can stop the process by closing your browser, but some mouse traps are so nasty that they require you to force your computer to reboot.

MP3   A digital music file that can be transmitted from place to place or stored on your computer, portable music player, or cell phone and played back. Technically, MP3 technology compresses the music to create a smaller file to allow it to be transferred faster or take up less space. Depending on how demanding you are, an MP3 when played back may sound noticeably lower in quality than a CD or DVD.

navigating   *See* **browsing.**

netiquette   A manufactured word meaning "net etiquette," the proper behavior and courtesy expected by most users of the Internet. **Flamering** in a **chat room** would be considered poor netiquette.

Nigerian scam   A general term for an attempted fraud in which a stranger (often from Nigeria, but also from other places in Africa, Asia, or Europe) contacts you and asks your assistance in transferring a large sum of money obtained in any of a number of hard-to-believe situations. In the end, the scammer will ask you to pay some expenses involved in the imaginary transfer or will try to get your bank account or credit card number and other information in order to steal from you.

off-line   When a computer is not connected to the Internet, it is considered off-line. The machine may be running and available for other purposes such as word processing or music playback, but access to the Web or to e-mail is not available. Your machine can be off-line because its physical connection to the Internet such as a cable is not connected, because its WiFi transmitter or **modem** is not turned on, because its Internet **software** is not set up properly, or because an Internet **browser** or e-mail program is not running.

online   A computer that is connected to the Internet by cable or wirelessly and that has **software** running to manage use of the Web or e-mail.

operating system   Software that manages the relations between **applications** and the computer's **hardware.** On PCs, the most common operating system is Microsoft's Windows; for Apple machines there are various versions of that company's OS.

opt-in, opt-out   Options offered to users of the Internet about whether you choose to allow (opt-in) or not allow (opt-out) certain actions by a Web site. These include the transmission of e-mails from the site, from other companies or groups that partner with the site, or from companies that buy your name and information from the Web site. At some sites, the standard procedure is to share information, and users must specifically request to opt-out in order not to receive e-mail.

P2P file sharing   A network of users who agree to share music, videos or other types of files with one another. P2P means peer-to-peer, a claim that the sharing is between individuals and not companies. P2P often involves violation of the copyright on entertainment or software, and users can end up being prosecuted. In addition, accepting files from strangers can lead to the installation of a wide variety of **malware** on your computer.

password   The code word, phrase, or number you use to confirm your identity when you sign on to the Internet, an online service such as a social network site, or to an e-mail server. The password is usually associated with a **user name,** and you will need both to gain entrance to protected sites or services. Some Web sites also ask for a **PIN.**

pharming   *See* **browser hijacking.**

phishing   A fraudulent e-mail or text message that attempts to get you to "confirm" or "update" your user name, password, bank, or credit card information. The term *phishing* is a computer hacker's version of "fishing" for information. Occasionally, a crook might even place a phone call asking for the same information. Legitimate online stores will never ask you for such information by e-mail or phone; they already have it if you have signed up for an account. Some phishing attacks will direct you to a Web site that imitates the appearance of the real Web site for a company. If you receive a message like this, either ignore it and delete it from your mailbox, or call the company, using the phone number you can find on their official Web site and ask them to investigate. A variation of the same thing is called "SMishing," meaning a phishing attempted by text message (also called SMS) to a cell phone or other mobile device.

PIN   A personal identification number, sometimes used as an additional level of security for Web sites, telephone banking, and debit or ATM cards. The PIN may be assigned to you by the company or service, or you may be able to choose your own. Never use something obvious like your own telephone number or date of birth; these are too easy for a thief to figure out if they get hold of your bank card or your online user name and password.

plug-in   A utility or mini-program intended to add new features to your Internet **browser** or other program on your computer or Web-capable cell phone. Some plug-ins are intended to allow display of sophisticated video or playback of music or sounds. Make sure that before you permit a plug-in to be downloaded and installed on your computer or digital device that 1) you have requested it, 2) that you recognize the name of the company offering the plug-in, and 3) that you have a current **antivirus** program running to guard against **malware** that might attempt to sneak in as part of the plug-in.

podcast   A digital recording of a radio show or other audio information that is made available over the Internet. Users can listen to a podcast on a computer, a Web-enabled cell phone, or a digital music player. The term comes from the most popular music player, Apple's iPod.

privacy policy   Web sites, credit card and banking companies, and other organizations are generally required to establish and make available their policies regarding how they intend to store, protect, and limit access to personal information about customers and members.

real time   Something that is happening live on the Internet. For example, most text messaging takes place in real time, with both ends of the conversation online. On the other hand, e-mail is often sent or received at the convenience of one side or the other in the exchange and not in real time.

router   A device that connects two or more computers or two or more networks. A router can be wireless, using radio waves to send and receive information, or it can be connected by wires to devices.

screen name   A made-up name members of social networking sites and other online locations can use to identify themselves without revealing their real name and location. It is generally not a good idea to use your real name or anything that would make it easy for someone to find you as your screen name on any public site.

search engine   A specialized type of Web site, or a function on a Web page that allows you to search the Internet for information of all sorts using **keywords** or phrases. A general search, like "baseball," might turn up hundreds of thousands of matches. More specific searches, like "baseball left-handed shortstop" will allow you to find information even quicker. The most common search engines include google.com and live.com.

server   A computer or hard disk that holds a shareable program or file (including music, video, or data) that can be accessed by other users. Many schools, offices, and organizations are set up to share programs and data in this way, and they obtain licenses from the makers of the programs and install security **software** to protect users. Some software and file-sharing services also use a server to hold information, although the files may not be authorized by copyright holders for use in this way, and the files that are shared may be infected with **viruses,** spyware, or **adware.**

SMS   Short Messaging Service is the technical name for the protocol used for most **text messaging** services.

social networking site   A Web site intended to help people meet people who share common interests or backgrounds. Sometimes known as "friend-of-a-friend" sites. Examples include Facebook, Friendster, and MySpace. Members can put a picture and other information about themselves; social networking sites usually offer ways for young people to keep their real names, phone numbers, and locations hidden behind a **screen name.** *Threats*: sexual predators, criminals seeking to steal money by obtaining credit card or banking information, and posers who are not whom they claim to be.

software   Programs and utilities written to perform certain functions on a computer or other digital device. For example, a word processor is software. The software generally needs to have a compatible **operating system** that translates its commands to work with the **hardware** that physically makes up your computer, cell phone, or other device.

software piracy The illegal copying, sale, or sharing of computer programs that are protected by copyright or other laws. Not only is piracy illegal, but installing an unofficial copy of a program is a common way that computers become infected by **viruses.** Pirated software is sometimes called **warez.**

spam Unwanted junk e-mail, instant messages, or cell phone text messages. The name is believed to have been adopted from an old *Monty Python* skit in which the only item on a restaurant's menu was Spam, which in case it's not on your diet, is canned and processed meat.

spim Unsolicited instant messages sent to users of services like AIM or Windows Live Messenger. The messages may contain links to adult sites, gambling sites, or to Web pages that contain **viruses** that will attempt to install on your computer automatically.

spoofing An action by a criminal to substitute a phony Web site or e-mail for a legitimate communication from a real company. Spoofing is usually done in an attempt to gain your personal and banking information, although sometimes it is done as a true spoof like substituting a parody page for the real thing.

streaming The process where content, including music and video, is delivered directly to your computer, cell phone, or other digital device for immediate listening or viewing. By contrast, the same sort of material can also be sent to your computer or other device as a file to be stored and played back at a later time.

surfing *See* **browsing.**

temporary files Many Internet Web sites download files including pictures, icons, and sounds to your computer each time you visit. Although this may add a few seconds to the time it takes when you first open a page, having these files on your computer will make it faster to use the page once it is loaded. For example, if you go deep into the pages of a Web site and then return to its **home page,** most of the elements of the home page may already be available on your machine. As a user, you should be aware that having these temporary files on your computer can allow someone to see what pages you have visited recently. And the amount of material stored on your computer may build up to the point that it slows down operations. You can adjust the amount of available space for temporary files within most Internet **browsers,** and you can also clear out the files with a setting in the browser or in your security software.

text messaging A means of sending short messages between cell phones and other portable digital devices. If a cell phone is capable of going on to the Web, it could be exposed to inappropriate content or to **malware** if the user clicks on a **link** to a Web site included in the message.

Trojan Horses A form of **malware** that appears to be legitimate, but once downloaded or installed on a program they can work from the inside to cause damage to files or make the computer do things the user does not want to happen.

URL The Uniform Resource Locator is the technical name for the Web **address** of a particular site. For example, the full URL for Facebook is http://www.facebook.com. Using modern Web **browsers,** the http:// prefix is no longer necessary, and many browsers will also allow you to do without the www. as part of the address. The end of the URL, which can include .com, .gov, .edu, and other codes tells you about the type of organization behind the name; the three just listed stand for company or commercial, government, and educational institution. Somewhere out on the Internet, a computer receives your request and translates it from the words you have used to the numerical address for the Web site. *See also* **http** and **www.**

user name The first level of identification required to sign on to the Internet, a Web site, or a particular service. In most cases, your user name is some form of your real name or a nickname. It is then paired with a secret **password** and sometimes also a **PIN** to help keep thieves and other unauthorized people from posing as you.

virus Any kind of program that is intended to cause mischief or damage to a computer. A virus, by definition, is intended to spread from machine to machine, either automatically over a network or by e-mail, or one computer at a time when it is installed from an infected machine or file. An **antivirus** program that is kept up to date should be able to detect viruses if an attempt is made to download them or if they sneak in and then try to take control of a machine.

Wapedia *See* **wiki.**

warez site A Web site or a file-sharing site that offers pirated or illegally distributed **software** (called warez and pronounced "wheres") for sale. Users of these sites may download programs that include **malware** or could end up in legal trouble if the copyright owner of the material obtains lists of users of the site and decides to file a lawsuit.

webmaster The person responsible for administering a Web site.

Web site   The Internet term for a destination or location in **cyberspace** where you can visit for information, communication, shopping, or other purposes. All of the Web sites of the Internet are linked together to make up the World Wide Web.

whitelisting   A highly restrictive form of filter that only allows access to Web sites or e-mail addresses that are included on a whitelist that you create or that someone else (a parent, a school, an employer) puts in place. All other communication is blocked. *See also* **blacklisting**.

Wi-Fi   A nickname for most types of wireless networks, used to connect computers to one another or to the Internet, without cables.

wiki   A page or collection of Web pages meant to provide quick and easily accessible information, created by members of a voluntary group. The best known of these is Wikipedia. The name comes from a Hawaiian word meaning "fast." Although wiki pages are reviewed and edited by members, the quality of research sometimes is amateurish and may not be good enough to be used in school or other research. The Wapedia is a smaller version of Wikipedia intended for use on portable devices such as Web-enabled cell phones.

World Wide Web   *See* **www**.

worm   A form of **virus** that is designed to spread from computer to computer automatically.

www   The first part of a Web address retains the initials of the original name for the Internet, the World Wide Web.

Zip file   A Zip file is a document that has been squeezed to make it smaller so that it can move over the Internet faster and take up less space on a hard drive. The "zipping" uses computer intelligence to find ways to remove unnecessary characters. Just as an example, picture files are usually quite large because they contain individual descriptions of millions of locations on the screen. But think of a picture taken at the beach; half of the image might consist of blue sky with just a few clouds. A zipped file might remove most of those individual picture elements (called pixels) and instead rewrite the file to say: "The next 10,123 pixels are all aqua blue." That's just one way a zipped file is compressed. Most modern operating systems are able to accept a zipped file and then unzip it to its full size so you can use it. Make sure you have an up-to-date **antivirus** program so that it can be on guard against a **virus** that is hidden in a Zip file and only becomes active when unzipped.

zombie drone   A form of **bot** that allows a **hacker** remote control of a computer.

APPENDIX 1

Helpful Organizations

Center for Internet Addiction Recovery
http://www.netaddiction.com

The MacArthur Foundation
http://www.digitallearning.macfound.org

GOVERNMENT AGENCIES
Federal Trade Commission: Consumer Response Center
(877) FTC-HELP [382-4357]
http://www.ftc.gov

Federal Communications Commission: Cell Phone Complaints
(888) 225-5322
http://www.fcc.gov/cgb/complaints.html

Internet Fraud Complaint Center

Federal Bureau of Investigation and the National White Collar Crime Center
http://www.ic3.gov

Phonebusters (Canada)
(888) 495-8501
http://www.phonebusters.com

Competition Bureau (Canada)
http://www.competitionbureau.gc.ca

Federal Trade Commission: Identity Theft
http://www.ftc.gov/idtheft

International Consumer Protection and Enforcement Network
http://www.econsumer.gov

National Do Not Call Registry
http://www.DoNotCall.gov

Secret Service: Field Offices
http://www.secretservice.gov/field_offices.shtml

U.S. Department of State: Advisories
http://www.state.gov/www/regions/africa/naffpub.pdf

ANTIVIRUS AND SECURITY SOFTWARE
Norton products from Symantec Corporation
http://www.symantec.com

McAfee, Inc
http://www.mcafee.com

Kaspersky Lab
http://usa.kaspersky.com

Bitdefender
http://www.bitdefender.com

APPENDIX 2

Text Message Lingo

The tiny keypads on cell phones, as well as the general interest of all young people to find quicker and easier ways to do just about anything, resulted in an entirely new language, or at least a new dialect. If you don't know the meaning of a word, there are dictionaries on the Internet, or you can type an abbreviation in a search engine like Google and find an entry with the definition. Here are some of the most popular ones. Some are fun, some are scary, and some are advanced early warnings of the presence of parents and other adults.

PARENTAL UNIT WARNINGS

AITR	Adult in the room
CD9	Code 9, parents are near
MOS	Mom over shoulder
P911	Parent emergency
PAW	Parents are watching
PIR	Parent in room
POS	Parent over shoulder
PLOS	Parents looking over shoulder
PRW	Parents are watching

GETTING TOGETHER

MIRL	Meet in real life
LMIRL	Let's meet in real life
WTGP	Want to go private (private chat)

SEX AND DRUGS

E or X	Ecstasy (the drug)
LGH	Let's get high
LH6	Let's have sex

LHSX   Let's have sex
TDTM   Talk dirty to me

ABOUT ME OR YOU

121	One-to-one (invitation for private chat)
A/S/L	Age/sex/location
ASLA	Age/sex/location/availability
BF	Boyfriend
BF	Best friend
BFF	Best friends forever
BFFL	Best friends for life
CWOT	Complete waste of time
CWYL	Chat with you later
GF	Girlfriend
ILU	I love you
ILY	I love you
KISS	Keep it simple, stupid
KIT	Keep in touch
MOOS	Member of the opposite sex
MorF	Male or female

JUST TALKING

411	Information or latest news
AAK	Asleep at keyboard
BRB	Be right back
GTG	Got to go
IDK	I don't know
LOL	Laugh out loud
Noob	A newbie. Someone new, or someone who is clueless
NMU	Not much, you?
NOYB	None of your business
NP	No problem
OMG	Oh my God
RME	Rolling my eyes
W/E	Whatever
WTF	What the ****?
?4U	I have a question for you

READ MORE ABOUT IT

Craigslist. "Personal Safety Tips." Available online. URL: http://www.craigslist.org/about/scams.

Ebay. "Marketplace Safety Tips." Available online. URL: http://pages.ebay.com/securitycenter/mrkt_safety.html.

Eharmony. "Safety Tips." Available online. URL: http://www.eharmony.com/safety/tips.

Monster.com. "Security Center." Available online. URL: http://help.monster.com/besafe/.

Young, Kimberly. *Caught in the Net: How to Recognize the Signs of Internet Addiction—and a Winning Strategy for Recovery.* New York: Wiley, 1998.

INDEX

A

academic credentials, online posting 44
ActiveX 112
addiction, Internet 4–5, 6–9, 139–140
address book, cell phone 124
adult assistance 11
adults-only Web sites 83
adware 51, 52
age, true disclosure 16
Amazon 24, 28
   Amazon Marketplace 24
antivirus programs 31, 54, 104–105, 107–108
AOL Personals 76
attorney generals, state 94
auctions, online 24-32
   auction process, online 29
   bid siphoning 32
   buy it now 29
   deadline 29
   online risks 26–32
   reserve price 29
   second-chance scams 32
   shill bidding 32
   spoofs 31–32

B

Badoo 13
Banking 18, 136
   frauds 18
   secure Web sites 136
Bebo 19
bid siphoning, auctions 32
BitTorrent 53

Blackberry 116
black market drugs 72–73
blocking 19, 123
   phone calls 123
   users 19
Bluetooth networks 120
brick and mortar stores 23
broadband network 135
browser, Web 31, 54, 136–137
   hijackers 54
   portable for security 136–137

C

caller ID, telephone 121–123, 129
Canadian Phonebusters Web site 35
Capital One 114
Careerbuilder.com 42
cell phones 10, 116–133
   address book 124
   advanced phones 116–120
   bills 126–127
   call records 10
   dangers 10, 116–133
   loss 120–121, 122
   safe disposal 128
Center for Internet Addition Recovery 4–5, 6–9
certified online pharmacies 74
check overpayment scams 36–37
Chrome, Google. See browser
classified ads 24–25, 38
Classmates 19
college admissions 15
Columbia University 73
Competition Bureau, Canada 62

Consumer Sentinel Network 131
  See also Federal Trade
    Commission
cookies, Internet 10
copyright protection 48–49, 54
Craigslist 25, 33–37, 42, 43, 76,
  Newmark, Craig 33
  scams 35–37
credit card 30, 57, 88–92, 125
  encoding numbers in a record
    125
  fraud 88–92
  protections 30, 57
credit reports 92–93, 95
  cleaning up bad reports 92–93
cross-border e-mail scams 57–62
cyberspace, definition vii–viii

D

dating 75–85
  safety tips, online 77–85
  services, online 75–85
debit card 30, 39, 57
  protections 30, 57
Department of State, U.S. 62
DoNotCall.gov 130–131
drivers license, online posting 39
drug sales, Internet 18, 71–74
Dumpster divers 89

E

eBay 24, 25, 28, 31
  Kijiji 25
  PayPal 24, 30
  Skype 25
  StubHub 25
eCRUSH 76–77
eHarmony 77–79
  eHarmony.com 77–79
e-mail vii, 55–70, 84, 111–113
  Cyberspace vii
  dangers 111–113

scams 55–70
signatures 84
Equifax, credit reporting agency 95
  equifax.com 95
Experian, credit reporting agency 95
  experian.com 95

F

Facebook 13, 15, 18, 19, 20, 21,
  41–42, 43, 53
  membership 18
  privacy settings 21
  profile 19, 20, 41–42
  security settings 15
FBI. *See* Federal Bureau of
  Investigation
FCC. *See* Federal Communications
  Commission
FDA. *See* Food and Drug
  Administration
Federal Bureau of Investigation 35
Federal Communications Commission
  122
Federal Do Not Call list 130–131
  donotcall.gov 130–131
Federal Trade Commission 35, 45,
  46, 60, 62, 87, 93, 94, 131
  advice to consumers 35, 46
  credit reports 93
  fraudulent job ads 45
  ftc.gov 35
  identity theft 62, 87, 93, 94
  Nigerian scams 60
  phone fraud 131
file-sharing 48–54
  involvement in virus spread
    101
Firefox, Mozilla. *See* browser
firewall, computer 103–104
flagging comments 19
Food and Drug Administration, U.S.
  71
4-1-9 scams 58–62

fragmentation, computer disk drive
106
Franklin, Benjamin 1–2
See also Postal Inspection Service
fraud 45, 95–96, 127–133
alert, credit report companies
95–96
cell phone 127–133
job ads 45
freeware 113–115
friends, helping with Internet danger
138–140
Friendster 19, 41
FTC. *See* Federal Trade Commission

G

gadgets, social networks 21
gaps, resume 45
Google Chrome. *See* browser
gray market sales 27, 72

H

Habbo 19
handling charges 28
hateful comments 16
history, Internet 10

I

identification verification services
79, 80
identity theft 86–99
filing identity theft report
93–95
instant messaging dangers 82,
116–133
intellectual property 48–49
International Consumer Protection
and Enforcement Network 62
international scams 57–66
Internet Addiction Test 6–9, 139
Internet cafes, danger in use 110,
135–136

Internet Explorer, Microsoft. *See*
browser
Internet Fraud Complaint Center 35
intervention, addiction 139
iPhone 116
Ito, Mizuko 2–3
iTunes 24

J

job hunting, online 38–47
academic credentials 44
application, online 10, 41
classified ads 24–25, 38
gaps in employment 45–46
references 44–45

K

Kazaa 53
keyloggers 50
Kijiji 25

L

LimeWire 53
links, Internet 109–115
lottery scams 62–64

M

MacArthur Foundation 2–3
Madoff, Bernie 69
malware. *See* virus, computer. *See*
also adware. *See also* spyware
Mangiacotti, Pat 80
master password vault 98–99
match.com 77–78, 82, 83
Meier, Megan 11
memory, computer. *See* RAM
Microsoft Internet Explorer. *See*
browser
misaddressed package scam 64–66
Miscellaneous Incident Report, police
95

MLM *See* multilevel marketing, *or* pyramid schemes
Monster.com 39–40, 43
Mozilla Firefox. *See* RAM
multilevel marketing 68–70
MySpace 11, 13, 15, 18, 19, 20, 21, 41–42
    hoax 11

N

NABP. *See* National Association of Boards of Pharmacy
Napster 49
National Association of Boards of Pharmacy 74
National Do Not Call Registry 130–131
National White Collar Crime Center 35
net addiction 6–9
    netaddiction.com 9
networking, social 14–22
Newmark, Craig 33
    Craigslist 25, 33–37, 42, 43, 76,
Nigerian scams 58–62
900 telephone numbers 83
Norton Internet Security. *See* antivirus
Norton 360. *See* antivirus

O

online now icon 20
online retailers 23–24
operating system, computer 102–103
    patch, operating system 103
Orkut 19
Othello 87

P

P2P. *See* peer-to-peer networks
Passwords 29, 39, 90, 96–98
    creating a safer code 90, 96–98

online 29, 39, 90, 96–99, 125
    reset trap 98
    vault 98–99
patch, operating system 103
payment, online 29–30, 34
    credit cards 30
    debit cards 30
    money order 30
    PayPal 24, 29, 40, 34–35
    wire transfer 30, 34
PayPal 24, 29, 40, 34
peer-to-peer networks 49–53
person-to-person sales 24–25
phishing 18, 114, 132
Phonebusters 35
PIN codes 89, 96, 124
Piper, Tim 12
pirated software 28, 48–54
Ponzi schemes 67–70
    Ponzi, Charles 69
posers 14
Postal Inspection Service 1–2, 60, 91
preapprove comments, social networking 19
prescription drugs. *See* drug sales, Internet
privacy 14–16, 19–20, 21
    e-mail address 15
    profile 19–20
    public search listing 21
    social networking 14–16
    Web page 15, 19–20
public computers, danger in use 110, 135–136
    Internet cafes 110, 135–136
public search listing, social networks 21
pyramid schemes 67–70

R

RAM 106
random access memory. *See* RAM
reconditioned products 27
recycle bin, computer 106

references, job 44–45
RelyID 79, 80
replica products 18
reporting inappropriate behavior 19
reserve price, auction 29
resumes, online 38, 39–41, 45
rogue Web sites, drug sales 73–74
routers, wireless 135

S

St. Bonaventure University 4
scams 32, 17–18, 35–37, 56–70,
    109–115, 124–126
    cell phone 124–126
    Internet 17–18, 35–37, 56–70,
        109–115
    second-chance, auctions 32
Secret Service, U.S. 62
security settings, social networking
    sites 15
sexual content 17
Shakespeare, William 87
shareware 113–115
    involvement in virus spread 101
shill bidding, auctions 32
shopping online 23–37, 56–57
    handling charges 28
    online auctions 24–32
    online outlets 23–24
    person-to-person sales 24–25
    secure Web sites 136
    third-party stores 24
Short Messaging Service (SMS). *See*
    text messaging
signatures, e-mail 84
SIM cards, cell phones 118–119, 121,
    128
Skype 25
SMS. *See* text messaging
social networking 11, 13–22, 41–42,
    43, 53, 75–85
    age, true disclosure 16
    dangers 14–22

friendship-driven 2–3
interest-driven 2–3
privacy 14–16
public search listing 21
sites
    Badoo 13
    Bebo 19
    Classmates 19
    Facebook 13, 15, 18, 19, 20,
        21, 41–42, 43, 53,
    Friendster 19, 41
    Habbo 19
    MySpace 11, 13, 15, 18, 19,
        20, 21, 41–42,
    Orkut 19
    about social networks 11,
        13–22, 41–42, 43, 53,
        75–85
Social Security numbers, online
    posting 31, 39, 42, 47, 86
Software 27, 28, 48–54
    licenses 27
    pirated 28, 48–54
spam 127
    cell phone 127
    text message 127
spoofs, auction 31–32
spyware 50, 51, 52, 53
StubHub 25
sucker list, e-mail 63
suicide, teen 11–12
Surks, Jason 73
Symantec. *See* antivirus

T

telephone scams 1, 127, 129–130
text messaging vii,
    Cyberspace vii, 116–133, 157–
        158
    dangers 116–133
    lingo 157–158
    scams 131–133
    SMS 118

third-party stores 24
TransUnion, credit reporting agency
  95
    transunion.com 95

U

unsubscribing from e-mails 56
update, operating system 103

V

virtual memory 106
virus, cell phone 119–120
virus, computer 31, 100–108

W

Washington University 43
WEP (Wired Equivalent Privacy)
  134–135

widgets, social networks 21
WiFi 120, 134–137
    involvement in virus spread
      101–102
WiFi Protected Access. *See* WPA
WinMx 53
Wired Equivalent Privacy. *See* WEP
wireless routers 135
wireless security 134–137
WPA (WiFi Protected Access) 134–
  135

Y

Young, Kimberly 4–5
YouTube 109

Z

Zip files, danger in use 111–112
zombie, computer 107